Glory Came in
Amber Rays

*A Mother's Spiritual Journey
into the Heavenlies*

paula dickerson

CROSSBOOKS
PUBLISHING

CrossBooks™
A Division of LifeWay
1663 Liberty Drive
Bloomington, IN 47403
www.crossbooks.com
Phone: 1-866-879-0502

First published by CrossBooks 3/28/2013

ISBN: 978-1-4627-2597-7 (sc)
ISBN: 978-1-4627-2599-1 (hc)
ISBN: 978-1-4627-2598-4 (e)

Library of Congress Control Number: 2013904174

Printed in the United States of America

This book is printed on acid-free paper.

Written for God
in loving memory of my child,
Amber CarLeigh, and
for her son,
Brentley

Table of Contents

Introduction

"Do not err, my beloved brethren. Every good gift and every perfect gift is from above, and cometh down from the Father of lights, with whom is no variableness, neither shadow of turning." (James 1:16-17 KJV)

I have one child, Amber CarLeigh, who brought pure joy to my heart and sunshine to my life from the beginning. We lived a beautiful life together for twenty-nine years, and then God my Father called her home to live in heaven. My heartbreak from her leaving was more than I could stand alone. I had family and friends who loved me, but God knew it would not be enough to save me. So He gifted me with glimpses into the heavenlies to help me live through the days when I did not know where to turn. With remarkable clarity, He taught me to look to Him for the strength and courage to live and move forward.

God did not leave me alone for one hour without the full knowledge of where Amber was. As my heart was breaking into a thousand pieces, He came so I would know Amber was with Him, and that He would care for her. This knowledge did not ease my tremendous grief of being separated from her; however, the message was so very clear that now, whenever I worry about her or question what happened, I immediately remember she is with God in heaven where the saints and angels dwell.

I wrote the happenings in notebooks and journals and on scraps of paper as a record of events to give to Brentley, Amber's little son, when he is older. At first, the writing quieted my heart and mind so I could breathe. I had always been a multitasker, and my activity level increased when Amber left. The constant activity helped me turn off the noise from the world so I could learn who I would become and how to live in the world again.

My dear friend Debbie Thomas drew me back to church, placing me in a seat where I could escape through a side door without being noticed if necessary. I needed to be in church, but I feared becoming emotional if I returned. So the side escape door made it possible. But as usual, I needed to multitask even while at church. As others sang praises and listened to the sermon, I listened and wrote words that came to my mind inside journals. These journal entries and my letters to Brentley about my visions and dreams became this book.

As I became stronger, I felt God wanted me to share pieces of these precious memories with other parents experiencing the death of a child. I believed that God wanted me to reach out to them and say, "Heaven is real and exactly as the Bible teaches." I usually did not know the parents or the child. Sometimes the sharing was done by mail, and sometimes I went to them. Why I was chosen to witness heavenly happenings I do not know, but I pray that sharing my story did and will bring comfort to parents facing this heartbreaking tragedy.

This is Amber's story and my story, which I share for God's glory. Amber always shined as a brilliant star. She was a living example of God's love, kindness, and grace. God sent her to me as a precious little bundle of joy and she became the sunlight to my days. She came from her Father in heaven and returned to Him when He called her name.

I had no choice in what happened. I do have the choice as to whether or not to share our story, which holds many precious memories that might help someone else in crisis and pass on information that might help one come to know God. My remaining silent in regard to others coming to know God—the most critical decision they will ever make in their lives—would prove I have no courage. My spirit cannot accept that. I want to be remembered as one who stood up for God in times of great trial. I have asked God to use me as His servant, and I pray for a calm heart and courage of words as I record these events. The spiritual happenings did not occur by accident. They came from God and the glory of our story belongs to God.

Some of the story resembles a near-death experience or supernatural occurrence others have witnessed when in the presence of a loved one as they died. These events started the month before Amber went to heaven and have continued through today. The story includes supernatural events revealed to me by God that are difficult to explain in our limited human language. The holy angels surely have a language capable of describing the beauty of heaven. I've done my best to describe these happenings, things I did not know before.

Please read these words with an open mind and a peace-filled heart. I pray that you will never again wonder if God and heaven are real. They are real and far more magnificent than what we can see or imagine on a normal day.

I understand that the supernatural events may leave questions in the minds of some. But I believe the supernatural is as real and active as everyday life. I live in great anticipation of seeing visions of heaven while on earth and then in the sky when I rise to meet my Father when He calls out my name.

God chose me to receive the blessings recorded in this story. Each event came as a new revelation to me. I researched Christian books and visited with pastors, Bible teachers, and friends for a greater understanding of the experiences I had witnessed. I studied the Bible in an effort to bring spiritual light to each event.

Over time, my research became more a pursuit of God and His ways so I could better know and understand Him. As 2 Timothy 3:16-17 says, "All scripture is given by inspiration of God, and is profitable for doctrine, for reproof, for correction, for instruction in righteousness: That the man of God may be perfect, thoroughly furnished unto all good works." (KJV)

In this book, I have included information for those who do not know God. I pray that your hearts will open wide to the reality of God, and I encourage you to read the Bible for strength to take the first step toward Him and the pathway to heaven and eternal life. God is watching and waiting for each person to choose to know Him.

♪♪ Music of My Heart ♪♪

Amber loved to write. When she was in fifth grade, she won a statewide poetry contest for her age level at Southern Arkansas University. I was so proud of her, and her poem thrills my heart. It has few words but carries a special message:

"Imagination"

A little child in its sleep, Dreaming.
A little foal chewing hay, Eating.
A little bird swaying high, Flying.
A little child waiting for food, Starving.

By Amber Davis
April 12, 1989

Amber wrote in her diary that winning that contest was the happiest day of her life. Everyone at school was excited for her, and of course, I was so proud of her. In her diary, she said she had considered giving up writing poetry, but after winning the award, nothing was going to stop her. God gifted Amber with the ability to write lovely poems.

I loved Amber from the moment I knew she was to be, and if it's possible, I love her more today. She and I always ended our conversations, saying, "I love you." It seemed the words were magical protection to keep us both safe until we were together again. The last time I visited Amber, our last words were "I love you." The last time I talked with her on the phone, our last words were "I love you." And those three treasured words remain in the heavenlies between Amber and me. Our love continues and will be the same when God calls me to heaven for a wonderful reunion. Like the day of Amber's birth, it will be one glorious day.

On a Sunday morning in October 2007, I was listening to the most magnificent music performed by the greatest orchestra. Each member of the orchestra seemed to be a first chair player. The intense music filled the air and was coming down from the heavens. Suddenly, I awakened while the music was still playing.

I attempted to explain in detail to my husband, Merle, the glorious sounds of music from heaven. I didn't say that I dreamed I heard heavenly music, as it felt much greater than a dream, as though I had witnessed firsthand the most wondrous orchestra. The music was splendid, magnificent, and classical—as though one had gathered together the most glorious orchestras on earth to play a beautiful song in perfect harmony. I remembered no singing, and I did not recognize the song. Later in the day, Merle and I discussed the music again. My feelings remain unchanged; the music came directly from heaven. Music has been an important part of my life but I had never heard a song that could be compared with the magnificence of this song from heaven. I now think of the beautiful sounds from heaven as the "Music of My Heart".

God knew what lay ahead and was beginning to prepare my mind and heart when I would face utter despair. He knew my heart would shatter, and He was moving closer to me, knowing I was unprepared for the event to come. God knows the anguish of watching the death of one's only child, and I imagine that He and the angels cried when Amber went to heaven. His gifts sustained me through many days and nights when I no longer believed I could go on living.

At the time, though, the music from heaven—created to glorify God—was magnificent and a blessing. Days later, I would cling to the memory of the celestial sounds.

Praise him with the sound of the trumpet: praise him with the psaltery and harp. Praise him with the timbrel and dance: praise him with stringed instruments and organs. Praise him upon the loud cymbals: praise him upon the high sounding cymbals. Let every thing that hath breath praise the LORD. Praise ye the LORD. (Psalm 150:3-6 KJV)

The music of the angels was created to offer praise to our glorious God. Music is the one universal language. In Revelation 5:11-12, John saw an enormous choir of millions of angels offering praise to God through their heavenly inspired music and writes,

> And I beheld, and I heard the voice of many angels round about the throne and the beasts and the elders: and the number of them was ten thousand times ten thousand, and thousands of thousands; Saying with a loud voice, Worthy is the Lamb that was slain to receive power, and riches, and wisdom, and strength, and honour, and glory, and blessing. (KJV)

2

♪♪ I Dreamed a Dream ♪♪

I spent the night visiting with my grandparents, Carl and Inez Gentry, who I loved completely. As a child, I had stayed in their home many nights in De Queen, Arkansas, but on this night, I did not travel to De Queen to see them. I traveled to their heavenly home, where they had gone years before.

The home looked different from the one they had when I was a child, but it was nice and cozy. We talked as if nothing sad had ever happened. "I Dreamed a Dream" in which I sat and visited with my grandparents. I cannot remember the words we shared, but it feels like we had a normal visit together. The love I have always felt from them lingered in the air. I loved them, and they loved me; a love that has not been broken although they live in heaven and I live on earth. Being with them again was so wonderful.

God wanted me to know that my grandparents are with Him in heaven, as I would need this knowledge for the days directly in front of me. "And if I go and prepare a place for you, I will come again, and receive you unto myself; that where I am, there ye may be also." (John 14:2-3 KJV)

3

♪♪ Turn the Page ♪♪

My cell phone was set to play "My Girl" when Amber called. I heard her calling and rushed to answer the phone. Instead, it was her husband. "Amber is not breathing," he said.

I remember screaming at him to save her, but I remember nothing else said. I called my sister and brother who lived close to Amber and begged them to go to her home and save her. I then fell to my knees, praying and begging God to save her. I'd get up, walk around a little, and then fall back to my knees. My only real hope was that God would intervene. I knew of nothing else to do but plead with Him to save her.

Thank God I was at home. My husband, Merle, was coming home, as he had been notified at work. Somehow, we learned that Amber was breathing and was being taken by ambulance to a small rural hospital. Merle and I headed for the hospital immediately.

An EMT at Amber's home asked my sister, Patricia, if Amber normally had one leg drawn to the side. Patricia assured her no.

The EMTs denied the request of Patricia and my brother Mitchell that Amber be airlifted to a major hospital. As a family, we had previously made this decision, never imagining we would be begging for this service to save Amber's life.

Instead, they transported Amber to a small rural hospital that did not have the capability of giving the necessary shot in a timely manner to limit brain damage for a person experiencing a stroke. Precious time was stolen as by a thief in the night. That time proved to be Amber's only opportunity to stay here with us. I cannot grasp why someone would decide that a person who had stopped breathing for several minutes did not deserve to be airlifted to a major medical facility. My family knew what to do if you have an expected stroke victim, and Patricia and Mitchell begged to have Amber helped in a meaningful way. It didn't happen. The minutes lost were lost forever. There was no way to bring them back.

The EMT's response was, "We have everything under control." It remains a mystery as to what she believed they had under control. Approximately halfway to the hospital, the ambulance stopped to pick up a person capable of inserting an intravenous line, which fully demonstrates that they did not have things under control. The 911 call to Amber's home was quickly and magically erased. No clear explanation was ever given to me, her mother, as to what happened on that day.

Later, Amber would be airlifted to a major medical facility, and every time we walked to her hospital room in ICU, we passed a large sign in the hallway that listed the procedures to follow when someone is suspected of suffering a stroke. Seeing the sign was heartbreaking, as we had begged for the things listed, but they were ignored, taking away any hope for Amber's survival. Amber had the human right to receive proper medical treatment, but it did not happen. Amber's case is a clear example of a patient's needs being ignored with devastating results.

With our emergency lights flashing, Merle and I raced to the hospital and to Amber. When we came upon road construction, the men didn't hesitate to help us get by. I can only imagine that we must have looked as stricken as we felt, and so they knew we needed help—an unexpected act of kindness freely given by strangers. Over time, this has happened many times. There are no words to express what one simple act of kindness means to someone's heart.

When we arrived at the hospital, a group of people met me outside, saying Amber was going to be okay. Many other family members and friends were gathered in the waiting room. My nephew Scott, who worked for the hospital, took me immediately to Amber.

She was not okay. I believe she could recognize me and desperately wanted to tell me something, but she could not. She also appeared to be in extreme pain. Since Amber was little, we had given each other three little hand squeezes when we were in a crowd to tell each other "I love you." I tried that many times over the next few days, but she never responded. What this one little thing revealed to me about her condition was devastating.

English was not the first language of the emergency room doctor, so communication with him was difficult. A nurse told me that if Amber were her child, she would get her to a large medical facility. Friends had already contacted the best-known neurosurgeon in Little Rock, Arkansas, and he had agreed to accept her as a patient. But for some reason, the attending physician would not agree to Amber being airlifted to Little Rock. Eventually, though, he did agree, and Amber was finally airlifted to Little Rock.

Merle and I left immediately in an effort to be at the Little Rock hospital when Amber arrived. We were speeding across the state toward a rapidly changing world.

Amber, Merle, and I arrived at the hospital in Little Rock about the same time that evening. Amber had shown signs of a stroke from the time she was still at her home that morning. Gone forever were the hours when she could have received the shot to reduce brain damage. The doctors worked to stabilize her so they could run tests.

After testing, a doctor called us into a small room and told us that Amber had suffered a massive stroke. The only reassuring news was since she was only twenty-nine she might overcome some of the damage. He said brain swelling would be critical, and that we wouldn't know for a few days how it would go. The doctor gave us this factual information without compassion. Never did he say a kind word to me. He took no action to relieve the pressure from Amber's brain, and he never discussed a plan of action to help her recover. The first time this doctor met my child, he began to play God.

At my request, my niece Shauna purchased a CD player and played the song "Ordinary Miracle" the entire time Amber was in the hospital. Amber looked lovely and at peace in the room, and the song reminded everyone that we were in a sacred place. A female doctor explained to me how grave Amber's condition was, and that I needed to pray to God for intervention. Thank God Amber had one doctor who believed He was there, listening to our prayers.

We were given a private room where immediate family could stay. It gave us space, but I knew in my heart it was not a good sign. Friends and family came from all directions.

A friend to both Amber and me called, pleading with me to do something to save Amber. I couldn't even speak. I searched through my brain for something to tell her, but there were no words. Knowing that I could do nothing to help my only child, the sunshine of my life, was beyond comprehension. My purpose in life had been to love and protect her. I could not comprehend how things had spiraled out of control so fast. I don't even know if I said anything. I think I just held the phone or dropped it, but I don't remember.

I knew in my heart that the doctors were not going to save her. In my mind, only God could help. Prayers were requested in every way friends and family knew to ask for them. Sincere, combined prayers by those who loved Amber were sent to heaven. I prayed constantly. Prayer in the chapel, prayer in Amber's room, prayer in the waiting room, and praying while trying to rest became how I filled my time. I prayed she would live over and over. I fully understood that if she lived she would have obstacles to overcome. But we had done that before, so I fully believed we could do it again.

Suddenly, we were in a room with a doctor telling us he was going to remove Amber from life-support. I begged him from my knees to not do this, but his response was cold and calculated. He said Amber's nurses, who were about her age, were struggling with this decision, and that other hospital staff was working with them. I never again saw the nurse who had cared for Amber the most. She and I had seen the small improvements that Amber had made. I will

9

never understand the doctor talking about the nurses when he was telling me he was taking my child off life-support. Did the nurses believe that everything possible had been done?

The doctor ignored my pleas, fulfilled his mission, and pretended he was God. Life-support was withdrawn, and Amber was gone. Although I was her mother, I had no voice in the decision.

I have often wondered if the EMT personnel and the doctors treated Amber as they would have if she were their child. The purpose of their position is to save lives. God knows exactly what they did and where their hearts were, and He will one day ask them questions surrounding Amber's care. But God knows the truth before they start creating an answer. Twisted facts around excuses for inappropriate actions will not be accepted as proof of innocence. With God's help, I strive to leave them and their actions up to Him.

A doctor who's name I never even knew made a decision to "Turn the Page" in my life to a life I could not imagine. He never asked my opinion. He offered no compassion. I have no belief he spoke with God before he did this earthly deed. Amber was taken away from me. My world crashed, and I was beyond reason. My prayers had not been answered. Amber had gone to heaven before me, but my mind told me that I was supposed to check that journey out first. I blamed myself for not praying well enough for God to save her. I did not believe she received the best medical treatment or that she was helped in that window of time when things could have turned out differently.

Invisible happenings were occurring in these moments. God was with me, and He was watching. "He sent from above, he took me, he drew me out of many waters. He delivered me from my strong enemy, and from them which hated me: for they were too strong for me. They prevented me in the day of my calamity: but the LORD was my stay." (Psalm 18:16-18 KJV)

4

♪♪ Angel ♪♪

For he shall give his angels charge over thee, to keep thee
in all thy ways.

(Psalm 91:11KJV)

Merle and I moved through the hallways of the hospital to the car and left without Amber. Though I had witnessed her critical condition for almost a week, I could not comprehend leaving the hospital without her. We started the drive home to Van Buren, the safest place we knew to go.

Grief was crushing my chest and mind. Who was I? I would never be called "Mom" or "Mother" again. I only knew myself as Amber's mom. I could not understand why my heart kept beating. I begged God to make it stop so I could leave with Amber. To die then would have been far easier than the days ahead. Normal life had come to a sudden, screeching halt. Our beautiful, safe life vanished into thin air.

Leaning forward in my seat, I covered my eyes with my hands. Suddenly, a perfectly square box became visible on my hands. Two angels appeared, facing each other and holding a brilliant, beaming golden light. As the angels moved, their hands worked with the golden beam of light between them.

The angels wore long, flowing robes covered with brilliant splashes of rainbow colors. Around each color, golden light rays beamed outward as bright as flaming fire. The angels themselves were a blazing light source. They did not have wings and appeared to be working with the golden beam of light in their hands.

God blessed me with certainty the golden beam in the arms of the angels was Amber. The angels were carrying Amber home to her heavenly Father. I knew she did not go alone; angels carried her there. God *had* answered my prayer. Amber "was" alive. God had my child with Him in heaven, and she was safe. A most precious blessing had come.

The glorious angels, living beings of light, were a glimmer of what heaven will be like. What a wondrous place heaven must be and we can choose to spend eternity there. This vision was the beginning of my understanding that God *had* answered my prayers. Amber was alive. I thank God with my entire being for this vision. I did nothing to deserve such a beautiful gift, but God sent it to me in my greatest hour of need because He loves me.

The Bible describes the appearance of angels as follows:

> Who maketh his angels spirits; his ministers a flaming fire: (Psalm 104:4 KJV)

> For by him were all things created, that are in heaven, and that are in earth, visible and invisible, whether they be thrones, or dominions, or principalities, or powers: all things were created by him, and for him: (Colossians 1:16 KJV)

And it came to pass, as they were much perplexed thereabout, behold, two men stood by them in shining garments: (Luke 24:4 KJV)

Merle and I had just gotten outside Little Rock when the vision came. He said I was sitting up and told him about it immediately after it happened. I also called Patricia to tell her of the vision, and that Amber was alive in heaven. On this day, over five years later, I pray to see the magnificence of heaven with this clarity again.

Recently I read this verse, "Do not err, my beloved brethren. Every good gift and every perfect gift is from above, and cometh down from the Father of lights, with whom is no variableness, neither shadow of turning." (James 1:16-17 KJV). I can imagine reading this verse in my past and not focusing on those last nine words,

"with whom is no variableness, neither shadow of turning." These words describe the angels exactly as they were in my vision. They were beaming radiant light from within. If I had viewed them from any angle, there would have been no shadow, as the angels beamed light outward in all directions.

God elevated my faith in the hours of my deepest grief to sustain me for the days ahead when He allowed me to see the angels ascend with Amber to heaven. I knew without doubt where she was, and that she was alive, healed, and cared for by God and the angels.

Death to a saved person through Jesus Christ is not death at all. Rather, it is a movement from an earthly life to a spiritual one more glorious than we can imagine. God allowed me to watch the miracle of Amber leaving earth in the arms of angels as she ascended to heaven.

As we planned the funeral and then attended the visitation and funeral, I knew that Amber was not in the casket. Neither the casket nor the grave ever held her. I felt no connection to them then or now. The grave had been overcome days before. As we were grieving together with broken hearts, Amber was with my Father in heaven. She did not go alone, angels carried her there. Today, my heart aches in appreciation to God for allowing me to witness this wondrous event. I do not know how a mother could survive after the physical death of a child if she didn't know where her child had gone. God rescued me from that torment. As John 11:25-26 says, "Jesus said unto her, I am the resurrection, and the life: he that believeth in me, though he were dead, yet shall he live: And whosoever liveth and believeth in me shall never die. Believest thou this? (John 11:25-26 KJV)

The invisible realm includes the host of angels in heaven that have immeasurable beauty and shine brighter than the midday sun. God created angels to be messengers or ministering spirits to those who know and love Him. God releases the angels from heaven to assist His people in fighting evil forces. Angels ascend and descend between heaven and earth at lightning speed to perform specific tasks according to His will. Angels are acknowledged in the Bible almost three hundred times.

God gave me a glimmer of what life will be like when I ascend with the angels to heaven to spend eternity with Him. The veil between everyday life and heaven is just a breath away. The spiritual world is within reach in every moment. The border is as sheer as a cool mist blowing in the breeze. Usually, we are not aware of heaven surrounding us, but if it's God's will, the veil can be lifted, allowing us a glimpse into the heavenlies. Angels are with us when

15

we are born and stay with us throughout our earthly lives. They are stunningly beautiful as to amaze those who witness their presence.

> Are they not all ministering spirits, sent forth to minister for them who shall be heirs of salvation? (Hebrews 1:14 KJV)

> Jesus said to the disciples, "Take heed that ye despise not one of these little ones; for I say unto you, That in heaven their angels do always behold the face of my Father which is in heaven." (Matthew 18:10 KJV)

> When the apostle Paul spoke of his own approaching death, he said, "We are confident, I say, and willing rather to be absent from the body, and to be present with the Lord." (2 Corinthians 5:8 KJV)

Imagine for a minute that you could see radiant angels surrounding you each day. Would it change the way you live? Would you be more careful with your words and actions? Would you become kinder to strangers, the less fortunate, and little children if you could see angels surrounding them and you?

May 14, 2010

Today as Merle and I attended the church service at Heritage Church in Van Buren, Arkansas, I noticed a man dressed in white sitting one row behind us. I did not recognize him. He was not dressed in a flowing white gown as one might expect of an angel. He was dressed in all-white clothing appearing as one maybe going to play tennis. When I turned around a few minutes later during the meet-and-greet time, he was no longer there. I searched the church but could not locate him. I wonder today, was he a man or was he an "Angel"? If it is God's will, angels can appear in human form on earth to complete assignments given by God.

> "Be not forgetful to entertain strangers: for thereby some
> have entertained angels unawares." (Hebrews 13:2 KJV)

The earliest known Christian paintings of angels show them without wings. The angels in my vision had no wings. After considering this information it seems normal. Why would a glowing being of light need wings to move through space? After the vision, I could not look at pictures or statues of angels without thinking, "That is not what an angel looks like." I removed all angel pictures and statues from my home and office and either stored them away or gave them to friends. The angels described in the Bible as having wings are called cherubim and seraphim. The word *seraphim* comes from a Hebrew term meaning, "burning ones." What lovely words, "the burning ones." Angels are burning bodies of radiant light.

> Then the glory of the LORD went up from the cherub,
> and stood over the threshold of the house; and the house
> was filled with the cloud, and the court was full of the
> brightness of the LORD's glory. And the sound of the
> cherubims' wings was heard even to the outer court,
> as the voice of the Almighty God when he speaketh.
> (Ezekiel 10:4-5 KJV)

One afternoon as I was driving home from Wickes to Van Buren on Highway 71, I met a large truck on a long curve with cars backed up behind it. In the gap between the cab of the truck and the truck bed, I caught a glimpse of a pickup passing the truck. I immediately moved onto the shoulder of the road. If I had remained in my lane, the pickup and I would have collided head-on. Later, while traveling on the same road, I moved over into the right-hand lane even though no cars were behind me. Soon, I met a pickup passing a truck in the lane I had just moved out of. I fully believe on both occasions that angels intervened and guided me out of harm's way. I believe that we will not know the many times angels have intervened in our lives until the day when we claim our rightful citizenship in heaven with God.

> "For he shall give his angels charge over thee, to keep thee in all thy ways. They shall bear thee up in their hands, lest thou dash thy foot against a stone. (Psalm 91:11-12 KJV)

Angels were created by God to serve God. Angels worship and praise God in heaven and intervene on behalf of His people on earth. Angels minister to God's people by the will of God. I am one of God's people and He assigned angels to care for me. The angels brought loving messages to me from heaven in the hours of my greatest need. They offered encouragement to my heart as it was shattering into pieces. They have protected me in times of danger. The angels cared for Amber as she lay dying a physical death and they carried her beautiful living spirit to heaven to be with God. Angels could do things for Amber of which I could not do. I thank God the angels cared for her and I thank Him for allowing me to know these things.

After Amber went to heaven, I searched for an angel description that included rainbow colors. Usually angels are depicted in white and having wings. Five years after I saw the angels I read the account from another describing an angelic vision similar to mine. General William Booth, founder of the Salvation Army, described a vision of angelic beings, stating that every angel was surrounded with an aura of rainbow light so brilliant that were it not withheld, no human being could stand the sight of it.[1]

Over one hundred years ago, General Booth had a vision of angels in rainbow colors as I had. What a blessing to my heart to read his words. As I write these words it is Christmas time. When I go shopping, someone is ringing the bell next to the hanging Salvation Army bucket, asking us to help the less fortunate. I will not walk past the bucket without giving from the heart. I've given in the past, but now it is such a blessing for me to place money in the bucket. The founder of the Salvation Army and I were blessed from God in the same way. How wondrous it was for me to read of William Booth's account of the angels in the rainbow light.

The heavenly events I witnessed came to me in time of great crisis. Life had brought me to my knees, and I fought a constant battle to regain my balance and move forward. The only one who could have saved me was God and He knew that before it happened.

The crisis was so big and out of my control that I did not know how to live. Amber and I lived in a way to not surrender in the face of a crisis but to go forward with God beside us. After Amber went to heaven it would have been much easier to admit defeat and just give up. It would have been a relief rather than something to dread. My constant prayer had been that Amber would have a long and happy life and would not leave this world before me. I will not get

---

[1] Billy Graham, *Angels God's Secret Agents* (Nashville, Tennessee; Thomas Nelson, 1975), 28.

over it in a certain year or time. I do know by choice I must learn how to live with Amber in heaven. Joy and happiness have come back into my life. Disappointments and self-doubt come, but I'm quicker and better at looking to God, listening to Him, and doing the work He sent me to do.

I have actually grown to a position where I have little concern about what others think or say about me or my work. That has not always been true, but it brings stillness to my heart and mind. I've been a grand people pleaser in my life. I've learned I cannot take care of myself or do God's work if I'm worrying about what others say and do. Thank God, He is helping me overcome this flaw in my personality.

It is a tremendous relief to just let people be who they are. Over time people always show who they are. More and more, I'm learning to trust my instincts in situations. God gave me those instincts for a reason so I need to trust them. I can hear God's voice much clearer if I'm not running around trying to do everything for everyone. God helped me grow into this new place. I thank God for sending this new confidence. I know I'm going to need it for the days ahead.

5

♪♫ Amazing Grace ♪♫

A few days after Amber went to heaven, a friend, Vicki Hall, sent me the book *90 Minutes in Heaven* written by Don Piper. In a note, Vicki asked me to read chapters one through three if I could read anything. At the time, her request was impossible. But later I read the chapters, and thanked God that Vicki sent the book. The words were astonishing, as they described events that were similar to what I had experienced. Though Don Piper's story and my stories are different, they support each other. Don wrote that he heard singing to the heavenly music; I heard only instrumental music.

Like Don Piper, I long to hear the heavenly music again. Sometimes in the middle of the day, it seems as though I hear a few notes of music playing softly in the background, which I count as a blessing. I have not heard the music again at the level it played on that first morning. I am filled with anticipation knowing that when I go to my heavenly home where God, the angels, and Amber dwell, the air will be filled with glorious music.

Music was always a part of our lives. When Amber was a baby, I played gospel, country, Cher, and Creedence Clearwater Revival while she was napping or playing. She grew up loving the same music I did. Amber wrote in her journal, "One of my favorite singing groups is Creedence Clearwater Revival which might have a relationship due to the fact that my mom listened to Creedence constantly while she was pregnant with me." I'm quite sure Amber did dance and listen to the songs before she was born. I love that!

When Amber was in college, a guy said in class, "Creedence is just a garage band." From her explanation of their after-class discussion, she clearly let him know that Creedence Clearwater was *not* a garage band, and that he didn't have a clue as to what he was talking about. As she was telling me this story I was thinking, garage band, what's that? Amber and I knew Creedence had been wildly popular when I was a teen and they played everywhere. They make me think of the Vietnam War because that's when they had their greatest hits. We didn't know what they looked like but we loved them. We sang their songs and danced away in our living room to the music. We were having fun while Creedence played songs like "Run Through the Jungle", "Midnight Special" and "Bad Moon Rising". Now that's fun. She was her momma's girl!

Amber was a confident young woman who was not afraid to tell the truth. If you didn't want to hear the truth, you didn't ask Amber. I'm so proud of her for being a kind, loving, caring, person who found gossips to be wasting time at best and hurting others with unkind words at worst.

When Amber was small, her favorite songs were "Oh Happy Day," "I Am a Promise," "Jesus Loves Me," and "He's Still

Working on Me." She was a brave little one and would sing solos in church as well as with groups. At home, she would sing the Charlie Daniels song "Swingin" verse by verse not missing a beat. She was country and proud of it. She didn't care if others thought it was cool or not. She was just my little Amber being herself. I can still hear her sweet, clear voice singing and laughing around the house, happy as could be. Amber knew how to laugh out loud, and it was contagious. Wherever she went, happiness followed.

We both played the piano and loved singing together. When Amber was little, she received a karaoke machine from Santa Claus and spent hours singing gospel and country songs. Sometimes we recorded duets. Amber's voice was sweet and clear. I enjoyed singing with her even though my voice surely was not as lovely as hers. By the end of our recording sessions, we would be rolling on the floor with laughter. When we went on road trips, we took tapes with us so we could sing while we drove. We didn't waste the minutes.

When Amber went to heaven, I could only listen to my niece Shauna sing "In the Middle of the Night" written by her aunt Glenda Blake. I listened to this song over and over, as this lovely Christian song calmed my heart and mind. I was driving many lonely hours each week between Wickes and our home in Van Buren so I could help take care of Brentley, and as I drove, I listened to Shauna singing. The words and melody are lovely and hearing Shauna's voice helped me feel she was near. In recent weeks, I realized that Shauna's singing voice reminded me of Amber's. So of course hearing the song helped me live those first weeks with Amber in heaven. Thank God I had that song when I needed it so much.

Shauna was born when I was a teen and it was great fun to come home from school, wake her from her nap, and play with her until she went home. I love her so much and now I feel it perfect how much she helped me through many hours of driving and she didn't even know. Amber and Shauna are like sisters. Neither of them had a sister, so as first cousins they became sisters by heart. They grew up singing special songs in church and for other events in southwest Arkansas. Many times, the songs were Christian favorites. That special bond between them will never be broken, and someday they will sing together again in heaven.

The next song that brought me such comfort was "Amazing Grace," sung by Darlene Zschech. Her voice is so lovely and peaceful, and it brought calm to my mind and heart. One day as I was listening to this lovely old hymn, I realized the fifth and final verse describes heaven as I fully believe it to be:

> When we've been there ten thousand years,
> bright shining as the sun,
> We've no less days to sing God's praise
> than when we first begun.

I knew with my entire heart that the author of this song really knew about Christians living in heaven, as he said they were "bright shining as the sun."

I began searching for information about the author and found that John Newton, a former slave trader, had written the song. So I read his biography written by Jonathan Aitken. The book describes a night in the life of this slave trader when he experienced a magnificent spiritual awakening as his slave ship was caught in a terrible storm. The ship was filling with water through a large hole in the side and was starting to sink. John Newton pleaded with God to save them. After he prayed, the cargo floating in the bottom of the ship sealed the hole, and they slowly sailed on to safety.

This event changed John Newton's heart forever, resulting in his becoming a great preacher and leading many to know Jesus Christ as their Savior. He lived in England and worked tirelessly to put an end to the slave trade. Newton died the same year the law passed, abolishing the slave trade. I believe God had His hand directly on John Newton as he sailed the slave ship, faced the treacherous storm, and cried out to God to save the ship and all its passengers. Newton knew that God had saved them. From that day forward, he lived the life God had sent him to lead.

Somewhere in the middle of the book, I learned Newton did not write the fifth verse of "Amazing Grace." Disappointed, I closed the book and placed it on the shelf. Later, when I began reading again, I researched the final verse. The author is unknown, but it is believed to have been a slave from the South. It would be just like God to have one of the slaves John Newton transported to America write the final and most important verse of his song "Amazing Grace." Maybe they heard John Newton singing "Amazing Grace" on the ship and added a verse of their own from the heart. I'd like to believe that happened.

6

♪♪ In the Middle of the Night ♪♪

Amber's five-year-old son Brentley and I were at a swimming pool. I watched him climb out of the pool, run around to the side laughing as he went. I was standing in the middle of the pool, and he perched on the edge getting ready to jump toward me so I could catch him. When he jumped, I couldn't catch him, and he went much deeper than I expected. I had to swim down in the water to pull him up. When we reached the surface it was Amber instead of Brentley. She was laughing with water falling away from her face. When I pulled her into my arms, she was so excited and said, "I could see you, I could see you!" She appeared as about the same age as Brentley. I had a beautiful dream "In the Middle of the Night" where Amber was back in my arms for a few precious moments. It was wonderful to hold my little Amber again.

Close to when the dream came I found a piece of paper in our DVD cabinet having the lyrics typed with portions of the words typed in red. The song titles are, "When You Say Nothing At All" and "The Prayer". I don't know how the sheet got there. Amber had typed some words in red about God on her MySpace page to ensure they showed importance to her. I do believe Amber typed these song lyrics highlighting the following words in red:

"When You Say Nothing at All"

All day long I can hear people talking out loud

But when you hold me near, you drown out the crowd

Old Mr. Webster could never define

What's being said between your heart and mine

"The Prayer"

I pray we'll find your light

And hold it in our hearts.

When stars go out each night,

Remind us where you are.

Let this be our prayer, when shadows fill our day.

Lead us to a place, guide us with your grace

Give us faith so we'll be safe.

I have wondered if Amber could see me from heaven. I wanted to know she could, but at the same time, I was concerned. I believed that she would be heartbroken if she could see me trying to live without her. I do believe those in heaven see some of what happens in this life, but I don't believe they are affected by the happenings here as we are because they know the time will come when God will make all things right.

After Amber went to heaven, someone told Brentley she was a star in the night sky. The first time he told me that, I thought about it for a bit and decided the words were good for Brentley. So we often looked for Amber as a shining star. Brentley was so young that he needed visual reassurance that his mother was there where she could see him and he could see her. His mother is as a bright and shining star in a clear night sky.

7

♪♪ Knowing What I ♪♪ Know About Heaven

One morning, Merle and I had finished getting ready for work. As usual, we said good-bye to each other in the kitchen before rushing out the door. Suddenly, one of Amber's music boxes started playing by itself. The music box sits in a cabinet with a glass door that had not been opened for months. The music box played the entire song "The Entertainer" from beginning to end. I had never before heard of a music box starting by itself or at the exact beginning of song and stopping at the exact ending.

This particular music box has a glass figurine of a girl with long blond hair sitting beside a wooden piano. One could imagine that it had been modeled after Amber sitting and playing the piano. "Knowing What I Know about Heaven," I realized that the sweet melody played by the music box was a great blessing. Again, music came in an unexpected way to encourage Merle and me forward during the saddest of days.

I know God sent this most lovely gift to us. I believe God allowed Amber to make the music box play to help mend our broken hearts. Only God could allow such a splendid gift.

♪♪ Somewhere Over ♪♪
the Rainbow

I n the book of Genesis, God established a covenant with Noah and his sons, all living creatures, and all generations to come that He would never again destroy the world by a flood. He then set a rainbow in the clouds as a sign of the covenant between Him and earth.

Rainbows are mentioned three other times in the Bible, all of which reflect God's ultimate power and His faithfulness and promise to protect His own.

> As the appearance of the bow that is in the cloud in the day of rain, so was the appearance of the brightness round about. This was the appearance of the likeness of the glory of the LORD. And when I saw it, I fell upon my face, and I heard a voice of one that spake. (Ezekiel 1:28 KJV)

> And immediately I was in the spirit: and, behold, a throne was set in heaven, and one sat on the throne. And he that sat was to look upon like a jasper and a sardine stone:

and there was a rainbow round about the throne, in sight like unto an emerald. (Revelation 4:2-3 KJV)

And I saw another mighty angel come down from heaven, clothed with a cloud: and a rainbow was upon his head, and his face was as it were the sun, and his feet as pillars of fire: (Revelation 10:1 KJV)

On April 12, 2010, as I was leaving for work, I stopped by the center island in the kitchen to get my cell phones and purse. Something from above caught my attention. When I looked up, I saw lovely rainbow stripes three to four inches long in brilliant color across the entire ceiling in straight lines and about ten inches apart. Each small rainbow was dazzling.

The sun was beaming through the high windows in the sunroom, so I reasoned that the rainbows came from the sunlight bouncing off the light fixture in the kitchen. However, I could not reason away the ones over the archway coming from the sunroom. When I turned my head, I noticed movement above me. I looked up and saw many smaller rainbows above my head that moved as I did. They were beautiful and glowed in brilliant color. I stretched out my arm, and the small rainbows spread across the ceiling.

I closed my eyes to praise God for such a blessing, but when I opened my eyes again, every rainbow was gone. The ceiling was totally white. I have not seen a rainbow on this ceiling before or since that day. God sent a brilliant visual blessing to remind me that He was watching.

Almost two years later, on March 16, 2012, Merle and I were traveling from Arkansas to Gulf Shores, Alabama. At sunset, the sky was a lovely blue with a few white, billowing clouds. Suddenly, the colors of the rainbow appeared on a cloud. I called Merle, who was driving the car in front of me, to look at the cloud. The colors were brilliant and then vanished.

One Sunday afternoon, as we traveled to Wickes to take Brentley home to his dad, two small rainbow stripes traveled with us on the same side of the Tahoe where Brentley and I were sitting.

When Amber was in the first grade, she wrote this little rainbow poem:

"I Would Like to Be"

I would like to be a rainbow
And be all different colors
And after the rain stops
I come out.

The children came and read their poems to the fifth-grade students where I taught. Listening to my lovely little Amber bravely read her poem to my students was a special time for me.

When Amber was four or five, the Care Bears were popular. Amber had two well-loved Care Bears and a Fisher Price tape recorder. She would play the tape recorder and sing the Care Bear songs. I have a recording of her singing the following song:

"Cheer"

Rainbow magic light in the sky
Red and purple catching your eye
Rainbow magic brings you good cheer
You see it whenever I'm near

I love that I have Amber singing this song in her sweet little voice, and the words are perfect to this mother's heart.

Rainbows have come in the most unusual and special ways to encourage me toward God and heaven. The rainbows were a vivid demonstration of God's presence with the promise that He continued to watch over me. Each time I see a beautiful rainbow, I think Amber is "Somewhere Over the Rainbow," just a tiny bit beyond my reach.

9

♪♪ Face of Love ♪♪

Jesus said unto her, I am the resurrection, and the life:
he that believeth in me, though he were dead, yet shall
he live: And whosoever liveth and believeth in me shall
never die. Believest thou this?

—John 11:25-26 KJV

L ate one night, I lay down to sleep and turned toward
the bedside table. Immediately, a brilliant golden light
appeared above the table just inches away, and Amber's
face appeared with her golden hair swirling inside a glimmering
circle of sunshine. She was looking at me and smiling. She did not
speak. She was beautiful and a radiant being of light. To me she was
the "Face of Love."

It felt as though Amber was checking on me and reminding me
how much she loved me. A beautiful white butterfly outlined in gold
fluttered in the lower left corner of the scene. It was a wondrous
clear vision, and then it slowly faded away. What a blessing to see
my child again and to know she was alright.

This vision supported the first one I had seen of the angels with a glowing golden light in their hands. As I had believed then, Amber's spirit was the golden light the angels held. On that day, I could not see her face. But on this day, God allowed me to see my child's face. I thank God for this blessing.

> And they that be wise shall shine as the brightness of the firmament; and they that turn many to righteousness as the stars forever and ever. But thou, O Daniel, shut up the words, and seal the book, even to the time of the end: many shall run to and fro, and knowledge shall be increased. (Daniel 12: 3-4 KJV)

> Now Moses kept the flock of Jethro his father in law, the priest of Midian: and he led the flock to the backside of the desert, and came to the mountain of God, even to Horeb. And the angel of the LORD appeared unto him in a flame of fire out of the midst of a bush: and he looked, and, behold, the bush burned with fire, and the bush was not consumed. (Exodus 3:1-2 KJV)

10

♪♪ This Little Light of Mine ♪♪

One day, Brentley and I had a long conversation about being sad that his "Meme," my Amber, had left us and gone to heaven. I realized that if we did not live a happy life with him, he would not grow up to be a happy person like his mother. From that day forward, I decided things would change, and we would be actively happy.

In the beginning, we were pretending as if we were actors in a play. But later it became our new normal, as joy would walk into our home and remain for hours at a time. Brentley's little face began to shine with his beautiful smile, and the twinkle in his eyes returned. I could once again hold him and say "This Little Light of Mine" is shining for all to see." A child's sparkling face tells the world that they are fully loved. Brentley, like his mother, knows he is loved completely.

In 2008, Merle, Brentley, and I attended a benefit dinner for my niece Amy's little girl, Maggie Joe, who had been born with a heart defect. She had lived at Arkansas Children's Hospital for many months before receiving a heart transplant, which allowed her to come home. The community held the benefit to raise funds to help her parents with the tremendous costs of having a seriously ill child.

Merle and Brentley had lots of fun placing bids on different items. Brentley placed the winning bid on a red motorcycle helmet. The people living in Wickes are accustomed to holding these events to help families in crisis, so individuals run up the bids, paying more than the item is worth. The benefit was a great success, raising the largest amount in a single event in Wickes to that date. Maggie Joe is family, and we did everything we could to support the event and have a nice time.

After the event, people asked me how I could have looked as good as I did at the benefit. I do not remember my response, but I recall feeling as if my entire body had been shocked. I have learned a better way to walk and move in the world. But although I'm better, I will no longer be the Paula I was before—not the one others knew or the one I knew. That person is gone, and a new one is emerging.

Perhaps this is why many people find it impossible to live in their hometowns after the loss of a child. Putting a smile on my face and attempting to appear as normal as possible was a conscious choice I had made for Brentley. Merle and Brentley gave me a greater will to live, and I felt that it was important for our future that happiness and joy return to our lives. Brentley is most important, and Amber would want him to have a wonderful life. As for Merle and me, we will do everything within our power to ensure that this child is happy and well cared for, just as his mother would want.

Many did not expect me to live past the tragedy. It hurts me to think that if I appear "normal" someone might doubt that I loved Amber enough. One person I considered a friend told me I would never look the same, and that others would always see the sadness in my face. I am now determined that this statement will not be true. God was and is with me, and with His help, I am determined to overcome. God is great!

The kindness freely given by strangers has been amazing. One day, a young woman, Erin, assisted me in selecting flowers for Amber's gravesite and shared the most meaningful words with me. As I was checking out, she motioned toward a little flower arrangement for a baby girl and said she was making it for her little girl who had died eight years earlier. With great sincerity, she told me that what had happened in my life was never going to be okay, but that I would get better each day in living with it. Thank God she told me that, as I needed those words and clung to them in the days ahead.

That day, Erin was going to have her IUD removed. The next time I saw her, she was beaming and told me she was going to have a little one. The store closed, and I never knew the rest of her story. I pray she has a healthy little one to love and enjoy every day. I thank God for sending her into my life. Her words were so very true, and I needed to hear them from one who knew what I was going through. "Fear thou not; for I am with thee: be not dismayed; for I am thy God: I will strengthen thee; yea, I will help thee; yea, I will uphold thee with the right hand of my righteousness." (Isaiah 41:10 KJV).

11

♪♪ The Scent of Love ♪♪

An indescribable fragrance of herbs and incense has surrounded me on five different occasions: once at church, once in our kitchen, once in my car, once in my office, and once it came at the house and traveled with me.

On March 16, 2012, the lovely aroma came with great intensity. I call it "The Scent of Love" and feel it comes from heaven. Merle and I were preparing for a trip to the beach. Amber and I loved to escape away to the beach. We loved to walk and sit on the beach, swim in the ocean, and listen to the waves as they drown out the noise of the world. As we would be leaving we would be planning our next trip back. Our beach trips hold great memories. I still love to walk on the beach and listen to the sound of the breaking waves. It brings peace to my soul, though I miss Amber greatly when I'm there.

"The Scent of Love" started in the washroom, continued into the kitchen, on to the car, and traveled with me on a short trip to the grocery store. The scent was much stronger than before and stayed for a much longer period of time. A heavenly scent magnified the air, none of which I can identify. I imagine it to be the marvelous aroma of heaven connected to my prayers, the presence of angels, Amber's closeness, or the Holy Spirit. I am certain that it was not an earthly scent.

Fragrance, aroma, and incense are mentioned throughout the Bible. God instructed the people to use varying ingredients to create a pleasing aroma for Him. The wise men brought frankincense and myrrh when they came to view the baby Jesus in the manger. When Jesus was an adult, Mary washed His feet in nard, which filled the house with fragrance.

The Bible describes incense as the prayers of the saints or people who have accepted Jesus as their Savior. Saints are blessed by the Holy Spirit, not the decrees of an earthly church.

> All thy garments smell of myrrh, and aloes, and cassia, out of the ivory palaces, whereby they have made thee glad. (Psalm 45:8 KJV)

> And another angel came and stood at the altar, having a golden censer; and there was given unto him much incense, that he should offer it with the prayers of all saints upon the golden altar which was before the throne. And the smoke of the incense, which came with the prayers of the saints, ascended up before God out of the angel's hand. (Revelation 8:3-4 KJV)

> And when he had taken the book, the four beasts and four and twenty elders fell down before the Lamb, having every one of them harps, and golden vials full of odours, which are the prayers of saints. (Revelation 5:8 KJV)

Prayers and incense in Revelation 8:3-4 are used together as if they were one and the same thing. I want to believe that the sweet fragrances are connected to my prayers. I now offer prayers up to heaven often during the day and in the middle of the night. I know God hears them because He has shown He does. "David said the following in his prayer: 'Lord, I cry unto thee: make haste unto me; give ear unto my voice, when I cry unto thee. Let my prayer be set forth before thee as incense; and the lifting up of my hands as the evening sacrifice.'" (Psalm 141:1-2 KJV)

12

♪♪ Knowing You ♪♪

I was awakened by the sound of rushing wind. I thought it was early morning, and that Merle was leaving to run and his wind suit pants were making the swishing sound.

I opened my eyes. The room was bright as in daylight, and a man dressed in white was leaning over and looking down at me. Merle wears a white shirt when he goes out to run, so it seemed normal. I closed my eyes and then immediately thought, *Oh, something is wrong or Merle wouldn't be looking at me like that.* I opened my eyes, sat up, and said, "What is it?"

The man was beaming white light, making the room bright as the morning sun. He was Jesus. I saw His face, but I cannot describe His features. I believe this will remain a mystery to me until I go to heaven or Jesus' second coming. He was radiant in light and then slowly faded away before my eyes. The room was dark. For the first time, I realized it was still night.

> And he said, Thou canst not see my face: for there shall no man see me, and live. (Exodus 33:20 KJV)

Merle was next to me in bed, asleep. Immediately, I woke him and told him that Jesus had been in our room. We sat up and discussed this remarkable event.

Our room was filled with an intense energy. I felt as though every part of my body had been awakened and every cell ignited. I felt more alive than ever before. This feeling stayed with me for many hours. I was overcome with awe, as one would expect after a visit from Jesus. Again, I knew heaven was just a step away.

Sleep did not come again that night. God sent Jesus to me visibly and audibly in the stillness of the night. What a blessing.

> Bless the LORD, O my soul. O LORD my God, thou art very great; thou art clothed with honour and majesty. Who coverest thyself with light as with a garment: who stretchest out the heavens like a curtain: Who layeth the beams of his chambers in the waters: who maketh the clouds his chariot: who walketh upon the wings of the wind: (Psalm 104:1-3 KJV)

"Knowing You," Jesus, made the difference in my life. "Knowing You" is how I know Amber lives. You came. You cared. You saved me again. If Amber cannot be in my arms, I want her to be with You. Thank you, Jesus, for the many blessings you have sent into my life.

> Wherefore he is able also to save them to the uttermost that come unto God by him, seeing he ever liveth to make intercession for them. (Hebrews 7:25 KJV)

> And after six days Jesus taketh Peter, James, and John his brother, and bringeth them up into an high mountain apart, And was transfigured before them: and his face did shine as the sun, and his raiment was white as the light. And, behold, there appeared unto them Moses and

Elias talking with him. Then answered Peter, and said
unto Jesus, Lord, it is good for us to be here: if thou
wilt, let us make here three tabernacles; one for thee, and
one for Moses, and one for Elias. While he yet spake,
behold, a bright cloud overshadowed them: and behold
a voice out of the cloud, which said, This is my beloved
Son, in whom I am well pleased; hear ye him. And when
the disciples heard it, they fell on their face, and were
sore afraid. And Jesus came and touched them, and said,
Arise, and be not afraid. And when they had lifted up
their eyes, they saw no man, save Jesus only. (Matthew
17:1-8 KJV)

One night at the Living Word Church in Van Buren, Pastor
George Lynn held a prayer service where many prayers were sent
to heaven as people shared the concerns in their lives. My arms
and hands were outstretched toward heaven when, suddenly, I felt
someone from heaven take hold of my hand for a little while. This
was quite remarkable to me and instilled my belief that it pleases
God greatly for one to praise Him with upraised arms.

One morning while I was working alone in the kitchen, a very
clear male voice said, "Paula." It was Jesus. Knowing He was
right there beside me comforted me, and it felt as though he was
encouraging me to complete His work. I believe He was warning
me that there is much work to be done in a short period of time, as
we are marching toward that time when Jesus will return to earth.
Ignoring this truth is playing with fire.

13

♪♪ Friends ♪♪

Amber came in excited from a basketball game because she had met a cute guy, Glendon Youngblood. She wrote about meeting him in her journal. Fifth-grade girls tend to get pretty excited about meeting a new, good-looking guy. Amber and Glendon became "Friends". He was one of those really good guys she could talk to without having to worry about him sharing the information with others. They laughed and talked on the phone and went on a few dates in high school but decided they were meant to be "Friends".

When Amber went to heaven, Glendon's mother Claudette came to me. Her face is one of the few I remember during that time. I don't know what she said or if she even said anything, but she held me. We looked into each other's eyes, knowing there was nothing we could do to make things right. Claudette knew I needed to be held and loved, which was all anyone could do, and she did it. I will never forget her kindness so freely given from one mother to another.

Glendon had a son named Lyndon who became a close friend to Brentley in kindergarten. Brentley was invited to Lyndon's birthday party at Chuck E. Cheese's, and Merle and I took him. The kids had such fun. Claudette and I visited, and I felt so loved and supported by her. Toward the end of the party, Glendon told me how very sorry he was about Amber. His eyes revealed that he cared and knew I was struggling. He encouraged and reassured me that Brentley would need me. He was so kind to me, someone he really didn't know but wanted to help—a blessing of kindness from one of Amber's true friends.

Months later in the stillness of a night, I visited the home of Glendon's grandparents, Bryan and Helen Musgrave. Helen and I visited in the kitchen while washing the dishes and straightening up. The kitchen had many windows, and we could see Bryan working in the garden. His garden was quite amazing. He must have had a magical green thumb because all the vegetables looked perfect. Neighbors came by, and Bryan gave them vegetables. He was happy, and we enjoyed watching him share the harvest and visit with his friends. He never took any money for the food.

Suddenly, I was awakened from this most vivid dream. It had been many years since I had talked with Bryan and Helen in Wickes where they ran the grocery store. They were always kind and helpful to me when I stopped in to purchase groceries. I cannot explain why I had this detailed dream of Helen and Bryan, but I know I visited them in heaven. The home we visited in was not their earthly home but was their heavenly home prepared for them by Jesus. I felt there was some connection to their running a grocery store in this life and Bryan freely giving the food to friends in the dream.

I wondered about the dream because I had not seen Bryan and Helen for such a long time. My mind accepted it as a gift related to my childhood. I did not know it came as a message of grace sent down from heaven for Bryan and Helen's family.

The following week, Patricia called to tell me that Glendon had lung cancer. He was being treated in Little Rock, and the news was not positive. It was just unbelievable news. When I saw him at the party, he was the picture of health and happiness. Now I was hearing he was fighting for his life. It was beyond comprehension. Claudette and I came from normal families in a very small town, Wickes, Arkansas, and had known each other growing up. We all attended church each week. Our parents taught us right from wrong, and that God was real and alive in our world. I could not comprehend how we could possibly face the same reality of losing a child.

I did the best I could to encourage Claudette and her daughter Gayla. We messaged back and forth. Eventually, they took Glendon to a doctor in Dallas, where I fully expected they would find help. But I believe he came away with the same diagnosis and expected outcome. It continued to be a heartbreaking time. Glendon was very ill for months.

I prayed with all my might. I had doubted that I knew how to pray when Amber went to heaven, but now I knew a heartfelt conversation in the quietest place was what I was to do. One day, while I prayed for a continuous period of time that Glendon would live, I felt I was no longer connected to earth, and that I could feel God's presence. I sensed God's reassurance that Glendon would live. Feeling much better, I believed he would survive.

I did not have the liberty to tell Claudette. I wanted to, but I knew in my heart that I should not. One afternoon, I saw her and Gayla unexpectedly at a gas station and told them that I believed Glendon would live. I sensed they both believed what I was saying as I am sure they wanted with all their hearts to hear those words from someone. In the shock of actually seeing them, I had forgotten the feeling that I'd had to not tell them. When we parted, I had the strongest feeling that I should not have spoken those words.

Weeks later, the telephone rang, and it was Patricia. Glendon had passed away that morning. What a loss to his family and friends, as Glendon was a good and kind father, a precious son, and a Christian man.

I traveled to Claudette's home the next day. There were six women in her home, all of whom were close in age and had suffered the loss of a child. And the unimaginable had happened again.

Claudette and her husband, Gaylen, were shattered. There was little I could do to help, but I was there. I held her as she had held me when Amber left for heaven. In the silence when no words could help, we held each other tight. Again, I faced Claudette with both of us being fully aware there was nothing we could do to make it better.

At one point, Claudette said to the group of women, "You have all lost a child and lived past it. I will do the same somehow." I thought to myself, *Oh, how strong she is to be able to look at us and say she will survive.* When Amber left, I could not say that.

The feeling I had was to *not* tell Claudette that I thought Glendon would live because God knew what lay ahead. God knew that he would live, but in heaven, not on earth. Glendon and Amber were great "Friends" in this life. They will live throughout eternity as "Friends" forever.

The dream I had of Glendon's grandparents in heaven was much like the dream I had of my grandparents living in heaven. God sent the dream for a purpose. He wanted Claudette and me to know that our children are alive and well with Him, and that we will see them again. They will not come to us; we will go to them.

Why that information came to me about both children, I do not know. But it was a precious gift from God, a blessing flowing down from heaven, erasing all doubt.

I thank God for allowing me to know fully that Glendon lives in heaven. It does not erase the pain of separation, but it does provide great comfort to Glendon's family that they will be united with him when God says the time is right.

14

🎵 Angel Standing By 🎵

I was sitting in green grass, facing what appeared to be a casket on the ground with dirt falling away from it, which was odd to me. The casket appeared to be very old and made of stone or a similar material. Letters or numbers were engraved on the end of the casket, though I could not read or understand them. The casket slowly began to turn so I was viewing it from the side.

The lid of the casket slowly started to open. The inside was decorated with a lovely pink silk material, much like what we see at funeral homes today. I became overjoyed because I thought God was going to allow me to talk to Amber.

Four beings appeared and sat facing me on the edge of the casket. I know they were female, but I cannot describe their appearance. I imagine they looked very different from anything I have ever seen before, and that God has protected me from the memory.

I was suddenly awakened from the dream, which seemed very real and out of the ordinary. I told Merle I'd had a dream that was not a nightmare but I felt a need to get over it to better understand it. We didn't discuss it further because Brentley was with us.

Merle and Brentley left to run errands, and I was left alone in the house. Suddenly, I started crying hard for no apparent reason, which seemed odd. The tears fell for two to three minutes and stopped as quickly as they started.

I missed a call from Patricia, and then my mother called, telling me that Patricia's son Brad, his wife Linda, and their son Robert had been in a terrible car accident. Linda had a head injury, was going in and out of consciousness, and was very confused when she tried to talk. The ambulance and family members were racing to the hospital in Hot Springs. Merle and I immediately left Van Buren to meet them. Prayer requests were sent out, and mighty prayer warriors spoke sincere prayers from the heart to God.

When we were about an hour away from the hospital, my sister called to say they were all going to be okay and would be released from the hospital that day. Linda had a concussion, but she was awake and speaking clearly. Brad's arm and leg were hurt but not broken, and Robert was not injured at all.

The accident occurred when a car crossed the yellow line and struck their vehicle on the driver's side. The impact spun the car around, and the car traveling behind them hit the passenger side where Linda was sleeping with her head on a pillow against the window. The pillow softened the blow. The policemen working the accident and the wrecker service personnel were amazed that they lived or they were not injured much worse than they were.

Our family was greatly blessed that day. I believe God had an "Angel Standing By" who intervened for each family member in the car accident. God had been watching over our precious Christian family and had stopped great harm or an untimely death from happening again.

I discussed my dream with Merle and Patricia. I felt the dream and the crying had been connected to the car accident in some way. The following morning, I had a strong impression that the four beings sitting on the casket in the dream had guarded against anyone needing a casket that day. I continue to believe that was the meaning of my dream and that I cried when the accident occurred. If I am correct in this belief, this is the first time I've been given specific information about an event quickly approaching someone in my family.

I searched on the Internet for information regarding stone caskets. I found that wealthy families in the past used them. These coffins were not usually buried underground. More than one hundred stone coffins have been discovered dating back to the early part of the first century AD. Some are decorated with carvings and paintings. Those found at the Mount of Olives belonged apparently to one of the earliest families that joined the new religion of Christianity and are inscribed with dedications to Yeshua or Jesus. Others include the names of disciples of Jesus found in the Bible.

This was the type of casket I witnessed in my dream, an ancient casket I had not heard of before.

15

♪♪ My Jesus I Love Thee ♪♪

Today I drove to De Queen to pick up Brentley for a visit. He got into the car and was excited to see I had brought his Valentine's Day gifts. Our tradition has always been to give him some treats and a stuffed animal that plays music and dances or moves in some other way. He immediately made the little animal, a giraffe, play its song. As the music played, it stretched its neck up high and three hearts appeared that said, "I," "Love," and "You." He was happy with the gifts, and his clear, blue eyes were shining. He stayed with me for a while and then returned to his dad.

I started the three-hour trip home. As I waited for the last stoplight in Mena to turn green, I closed my eyes for a minute, and a lovely white butterfly outlined in gold fluttered into view. The butterfly twisted and turned so I could view it from the side and from the back. It had flowing tails, longer than a normal butterfly. Then the light changed, and I had to move on.

I pulled into a parking lot, closed my eyes again, and the butterfly was still there. I watched it for a while, and then it faded away. I am so happy that I took the time to see if the vision remained. In the past, I have thought that I did something to make the unusual happenings disappear, so I strive to not do that now.

This was the same butterfly in which I saw Amber's face after she ascended to heaven. I felt an overwhelming sense of "My Jesus I Love Thee" as I traveled the long drive home to Van Buren. I knew He was with me and that He knew my heart still ached for Amber. I love Him and He continues to remind me how very close heaven is.

16

♪♪ Brown Eyed Girl ♪♪

Amber had a sparkling Mickey Mouse denim jacket that we purchased on a trip to Disney World when she was a teen that she loved and wore often. After she went to heaven, I wanted to make a picture with the Mickey Mouse on the jacket. So I dismantled the jacket into pieces and took them to the framing department at Hobby Lobby. They had framed most of the other pictures in my home, so it was the natural place to start. Maybe because I didn't want to be questioned, I waited to work with the person I knew the least in the frame shop. Her nametag said she was Christa.

Christa was friendly and kind and immediately had ideas of what I could do. She showed me how I needed to work with the fabric pieces, and I took the jacket home and did the work. We did this back and forth a few times, and then I left it with her. I placed a treasured jacket in the hands of a lovely girl that my heart had trusted from the beginning.

Late on Christmas Eve, Christa called and left a message that the jacket was framed. I could hear the excitement in her voice.

When I went to pick up the picture, Christa brought it out, beaming with pride. The jacket had turned into a lovely framed piece of art. It hangs in my bedroom and feels as though it is exactly where it belongs.

Through visiting with Christa, I learned that she was an artist. It made perfect sense, as she had turned the Mickey Mouse jacket into a piece of art. Later I learned Christa had chosen to work the spring semester of 2007 at Disney World and completed the Disney College Program. I had placed the Mickey Mouse jacket in the hands of one who knew Mickey well.

I believe Christa instinctively knew that she was working with someone who had a broken heart, but she never pried. She was just caring and kind. I believe that the strong values instilled in her by her lovely Christian family allowed our hearts to merge before we even knew each other. God did that.

Christa was asked to show her art at an exhibition at the Van Buren Fine Arts Center, and she invited me to go. I was looking forward to seeing her pieces for the first time. But on the day of the show, I kept Brentley later than normal in Wickes and missed seeing her at the art show. I did go, though, and studied each painting and photographed each piece of art. I didn't know enough about the art world to know that was inappropriate. It turned out to be a blessing for Christa, though, because it is now the only copy of the artwork she has.

Christa's artwork is heavenly. Every painting is amazing, and it is impossible to say which piece is the most beautiful. Many of her first pieces of art were painted on old ceiling tiles from a school, as that was an economical way to paint for her.

Christa applied for the position of artistic assistant at the Van Buren Fine Arts Center. One afternoon, she called me very excited because she had been offered the position. As with many young people who are beginning a new job that has the potential to impact their lives, she was apprehensive. I tried to encourage and assure her that she could do the work.

Christa and I met for the first time at a little coffee shop in Van Buren. I shared information with her about Amber, and she shared information with me about her art. Though there is a large age difference between us, it felt as if we had known each other for a long time.

Christa told me her art pieces were usually inspired by a person, so I asked her to create a painting celebrating Amber's life. She was excited about the prospect and asked me to share more information about Amber. Later, I gathered a few pictures and other little treasures in a box and took them to Chili's where we planned to meet.

She came in all smiles, wearing the shoes I had given her as a thank-you gift for the lovely work she had done on the Mickey Mouse picture. After we ordered something to drink, I shared stories about Amber. Talking with Christa gave me the opportunity to talk about Amber with someone who had not known her, so she could respond without getting upset. On that day, Christa became my "Brown Eyed Girl." She listened with her heart as I shared my precious memories of Amber. Thinking back, I believe this might have been a lot for a young person to deal with. At the time, confiding in her seemed normal, but that was probably because I needed her more than she or I realized. We were brought together by God to love and support each other. It is a great connection of the heart.

A beautiful conversation began that day between a mother with a broken heart and a young woman with a loving heart. We started with memories of Amber, and our conversations have continued to this day. No subject is off-limits. Christa has learned a few things from me and has listened to the great joy of being a mother and a grandmother. And I've been given the chance to see how the young move and work in the world today. We share a strong Christian faith that began from loving families with a strong faith in God.

Christa was asked to show her art at an art show at the Van Buren Center for Art and Education. She needed multiple new pieces to show and sell. She started some of the work at our home, as some of her pieces are fairly large and I have the space where she could have multiple pieces going at one time.

Watching her paint was new to me, and it brought peace to my heart and mind. Christa would start a piece in the late afternoon and paint until the wee hours of the morning. The longer she works on an individual piece, the stronger her connection to God becomes, and late in the night, God guides her hands. It is hard to explain, but each piece stands alone as a beautiful piece of art I call "Christa Art." At times, she paints with her fingers. The end result looks like no other paintings. Others viewing the pieces recognize how unique they are. They may not recognize God's touch in the pieces, but when a painting is complete, it is always there. Christa knows God is with her when she paints. What a blessing.

Christa and her parents are new to our lives but feel like family. Christa and I have called her parents many nights, seeking knowledge on a particular subject, and they have freely shared. When prayers are needed, they are mighty prayer warriors for God. How wonderful that they are close during the toughest of days.

Christa is our God-daughter. She walks each day with God, serving Him in a most remarkable way. She came to me when I did not know to ask, looking exactly like a child I would have chosen. She has lovely dark hair and eyes. When I wasn't looking, I turned around, and there she was. God works in mysterious ways.

♪♪ How Great Thou Art ♪♪

I n 2011, I received a copy of my great-grandfather Wallace William White's written testimony regarding his life and belief in God. He was born in 1866 in Alabama and died in 1940 in Arkansas before I was born. I've heard many stories about him. He was the father of fifteen children, a hardworking man who owned a large farm where he had a flour mill, a sorghum mill, a twenty-acre blackberry patch, chickens, and cattle. He was the second American to own the land where my family still lives today. Here is his testimony:

Grannis, Arkansas
April 27, 1939

To whom it may concern:

I want to say the Bible says we get in return four fold for every kind deed we do. If you will remember, I have tried that kind of life. I have experience, and every thing has proved that it is true. If you want to and will, the balance of your days will be peaceful instead of troublesome. I want to say to all that are careless about obeying God to remember that every word that he says is true, and we will get what he promised and make our lives happy instead of troublesome. It has been on me for several months, enjoying the hope and good pleasure because I have hope in God also all the hard thoughts and feelings for every one have left me and love took its place.

Love and good will to all.

W. W. White

I am so thankful to have his words to read. They assure me that when I rise to heaven, I will meet a great-grandfather who I did not know in this life. What an exciting thought.

Great-grandfather White's testimony is proof that people should write their personal testimony to preserve it for generations to come. It can be shared when the person decides and can make a difference in the lives of many people, encouraging them to know and love God. My great-grandfather's words written in 1939 may be the spark that lights a fire in someone's heart to know and love God forever. "If it be possible, as much as lieth in you, live peaceably with all men." (Romans 12:18 KJV)

God is real and Jesus is His Son who once lived on earth. As a child, I believed this to be factual information. There was never any reason for me to doubt God because my parents, grandparents, aunts, and uncles were strong Christians who believed that God, Jesus, and the Holy Spirit were alive, real, and actively working in the world. I have no memory of ever doubting that God is real.

I was blessed to grow up in this family because living for God and moving toward God was the natural way to live. My childhood days were spent on the farm my great-grandfather White had purchased years before. As generations before us, God's beautiful nature was the perfect playground for Patricia, Mitchell, and me.

My father and mother, John and Imogene Tidwell, named me Paula when I was born. As a child, I did not feel this was a pretty or special name. After Amber went to heaven, God spoke to my heart, saying that the apostle Paul was very important and to study his writings. Now I'm proud that Paula is my name, as Paula is the feminine form of the name Paul. I like to think that, although my parents did not know it, they named me after the apostle Paul.

My family attended Grannis Baptist Church when I was growing up. When I was twelve, I asked God to come into my heart, was baptized, and became a member of the church. I was sincere and understood I should publicly acknowledge my belief in God even though my heart had loved Him from the beginning.

When I was in second grade, Trisha began taking piano lessons at school. We didn't have a piano, but we lived between two old country churches that did. We were given a key to each church, and so we walked to one of the churches for her to practice each afternoon. I watched her practice each day, and as a reward, she allowed me to play a song when she was finished. I loved the keys, the sounds, and the touch of the piano. In some unusual way, I loved the piano. We were playing in a little country church, and God was our audience. I imagine that God was smiling as He watched two little girls walking to church to practice playing the piano. The practice always included hymns written to worship Him. Today, I find this part of my history a precious memory.

One day my grandmother, Deloma Tidwell, located an older piano for sale in the newspaper for one hundred dollars. My parents were careful with their money, but I have no memory of there being a discussion as to whether they should buy the piano or not. Grandmother had found it and said we needed it. My dad obeyed his mother and drove to Mena, purchased the piano, and placed it in our bedroom. What a wonderful gift to a child who loved the feel of the piano keys! This was not just any piano; it was a baby grand piano, and it belonged to us. What a grand thing my Grandmother Tidwell had done for me.

A traveling piano tuner would come by our house every year or two and tune the piano. He wanted our baby grand and promised us a new piano in exchange for ours. I loved my piano, so his offer was always refused. He probably left confused that a little girl would turn down an offer for a new piano. He didn't know I was in love with my piano.

Today, the piano sits in the room where I write. Like me, Amber grew up learning to play on this piano. What fun we had singing, playing duets, and practicing for special events at this lovely piano. This was not and never will be an ordinary piano. It lives with me as I live with it. What a blessing located by my grandmother years ago. Maybe she knew what a wonderful change she made in my life on the day she asked my dad to purchase it. My heart believes she did.

Grandmother Tidwell lived just up the road from our home and would walk down to visit us, carrying her Bible on each trip. The minute she walked into our house, we obeyed an unspoken rule. Patricia or I would immediately sit down at the piano and play "How Great Thou Art." Grandmother Tidwell would close her eyes, sing, and wave her hands in praise to God. Other hymns would follow, but "How Great Thou Art" was first and foremost her favorite.

One summer day, I was playing around on the piano and played the notes to "He Arose" without sheet music. I told Patricia what I had done and she acted as though I was being silly. She said I had just played the song from memory and then ignored me. I didn't understand what had just happened, but I knew it was something new and different. The notes had not come from my memory; I did not play the song by heart. I just played a song without understanding where it came from. I was amazed. I knew nothing about people playing music by ear, but I had just done it.

Over time, it became a blessing because special music was not easily located in southwest Arkansas. If someone needed a song and we could not locate the sheet music, I would practice it by ear, write it down so as not to forget it, and play it for whatever event. It was a gift from God to a little girl to help the local churches and my school.

When I was in fourth grade, the grandfather of our church pianist bought the church a beautiful new piano. Before the next Sunday, the young pianist married her boyfriend and moved away, and the church was left without anyone to play the beautiful new piano. Someone contacted our parents and asked if Patricia and I would be the new church pianists.

I don't know how they knew we played the piano. I do remember my mother explaining to Patricia and me what we were being asked to do for the church. I couldn't really comprehend what it meant to be a church pianist, but I knew it meant I would get to play a lot and in front of many people. I would be the one to open and close the piano on Sunday mornings, a movement that felt sacred to me. I would be helping the church and making my parents proud. God would be with me, and I would play for Him. I was beyond happy, and my heart was singing. A dream had come true. I didn't know enough to be scared.

So I grew up playing piano in our Baptist church. The song leader would provide Patricia and me a list of songs for the following week so we could practice them before the next Sunday. God touched my heart as a child, and I tried to play music to please His ears. I could feel God's presence sitting next to me at the piano in church. He was there. God was watching.

I often played the piano for a small Pentecostal church near our home and for other churches for Christmas and Easter programs, revivals, weddings, and funerals. Playing the piano for many different churches and denominations allowed me the opportunity to hear teaching and preaching from many different pastors and church leaders. There were differences in the churches, but they were all Christian and the people were worshipping the same God. I never thought one church was more right than another. I knew God was there, and that was all that mattered.

God gifted me with the ability to play hymns. Then He sent opportunities for me to play the hymns for many churches. I was a guest in many churches, playing the piano for God. I answered God's call. At the time, I did not understand how much I should have thanked God for this opportunity. Today, I understand that it was in His control, and I was an instrument, doing His will. I thank God greatly for this blessing.

I taught Sunday school classes and worked in vacation bible schools. I led youth choirs, traveled with the youth to summer conferences, baked food for church events, and helped in other ways that were needed. God was always there beside me. I also started teaching the young ones when I was very young. At the time, I wondered if I knew enough to be teaching Sunday school. I pray that the Holy Spirit spoke for me when I knew not what to say.

When we were young, people would say Patricia and I were shy. I had a small understanding of what the word *shy* meant, and when they said it, I would think *I am not. That is not me.* Today, I am determined to have the word *shy* erased from any description of myself. God's work demands that I not be shy in spreading His Word. I plan to stand up for God until the day I rise to meet Him. No other one will have control over my hands or mouth. There is much work to be done for God in a short amount of time. We must not be wasteful of time or idle with our hands. "But the mercy of the LORD is from everlasting to everlasting upon them that fear him, and his righteousness unto children's children" (Psalm 103:17 KJV)

18

♪♪ Oh Happy Day ♪♪

Early in the morning, the doctor placed Amber, crying and wiggling, in my arms, close to my face. I loved her at first sight. God had answered my every prayer, and she was more beautiful than I ever imagined. My baby was in my arms, and she was perfect. I was the first to hold her, kiss her, and talk to her. She knew me, and I knew her. The love was there in the beginning and remains the same today. That great, miraculous day was Saturday, March 11, 1978. "Oh Happy Day" is the only way to describe it.

My mother and sister had gone with me to the first doctor visit when I was confirmed pregnant. We three decided that the baby would be a girl with blond hair and blue eyes. And she came exactly as we had ordered: a precious baby girl with shining blue eyes and light blond hair. She was the look of love.

I had waited my entire life for this baby. From the first day, she loved for me to talk to her, and she would look back at me as though she completely understood what I was saying. She would be so quiet and still. I sang to her as I fed her and when she was falling to sleep. I'm guilty of holding her for the fun of it because I wanted her close to me, heart to heart.

In the days leading up to her birth, we had been struggling with selecting a name for a baby girl. I had created a middle name, CarLeigh, after my grandfather Carl, her dad Carlton, and my middle name Carlene. The Leigh part of the name including the capital "L" in the middle, I just made up because I thought it sounded and looked beautiful. When I read Amber's diary she mentioned the importance of her middle name having the capital "L". She loved it like I did.

My parents read the *Sword of the Lord* magazine and attended the Sword of the Lord conferences in Murfreesboro, Tennessee, both founded by evangelist John Rice. My dad mentioned one day that John Rice had a granddaughter named Amber. When I heard that name, the search was over. Thank God the perfect name had come. My heart was singing. Amber sounded lovely, and it fit perfectly with CarLeigh. She would be Amber CarLeigh.

The color amber is found in the Bible in the book of Ezekiel. Its use demonstrates God's overbearingly bright and immediate presence. How wonderful that this color became my baby's name! She was a bright and shining star wherever she went on earth, and she is now shining as the sun in heaven. Her beautiful amber-colored hair framed her lovely face on earth and continues to do so in heaven. God planned that.

God sent her straight to my arms from heaven. I didn't follow the rules made by another on how to be a mother. I raised her my way. My way was to pick and choose behavior I had seen other parents use, including my own parents, and then when in doubt of their methods, I made up my own. Thank God I had enough confidence to make my own choices. From the first day she and I talked and talked. We spoke the language of love from the start. Love lived right there between us without a gap. Today it is still there, living in the air between us.

As a child I wanted to be held and loved by my mother. I was never happier than when I was with my mother. She and I talked about important things. Mom was always on my side. She was a beautiful example of a loving mother.

When Amber came I held her and loved her. I was determined Amber would know every day she was loved completely. I wanted her to know she was beautiful. Amber was a kind little soul, secure in the knowledge that she was surrounded by people who loved her. Knowing she was fully loved gave her security and confidence as she lived each day. The following Scripture gives us a beautiful definition of love freely given without conditions:

> Love is patient, love is kind. It does not envy, it does not boast, it is not proud. It does not dishonor others, it is not self-seeking, it is not easily angered, it keeps no record of wrongs. Love does not delight in evil but rejoices with the truth. It always protects, always trusts, always hopes, always perseveres. Love never fails. (1 Corinthians 13:4-8 NIV)

I am so thankful that from the beginning Amber and I made the most of every day. We didn't know how short our time on earth together would be, and I can say from the heart that we made the moments matter. From the tiniest little thing during a normal day live the sweetest memories.

Amber and I were kindred spirits. Our love relationship started the day she was born and continues through this day. We had a secret love language where, in a few words or none at all, we could convey to each other what was happening or needed.

Over the years, Amber and I made up a rule that you don't let the public know when you are hurting in any way. We made this plan out loud and we lived it. On most days, the rule worked well but then the big special days started coming. Graduation Day from high school was going to be a challenge. Amber reminded me I was absolutely *not* to cry. Amber gave me a bouquet of lovely roses and a card with "Thelma and Louise" written on the envelope. I peeked into the envelope, realized it was a mistake, and quickly closed the card and pretended it wasn't there. When we had watched the movie "Thelma and Louise" Amber had decided we were the two main characters. It was impossible for me to read the card and mind the rule. I didn't shed a public tear on this grand day.

Later by myself, I read the card and teardrops fell. They were happy little tears because I was so proud of Amber's accomplishments in school and the way she chose to live her life. Amber's graduation was an "Oh Happy Day" and many special memories were made. She always thought it was funny that she had given me "the card" in the middle of a crowd expecting me to not cry.

On the day she was married, Amber put the same rule in place for the entire day. I was a good mother and did not shed a tear. We also made a new rule for the wedding day. This was a day for happiness, so no matter what unexpected thing happened it was not to ruin our day. And unexpected things happened. The preacher was running late. It started raining, so the girls had to

71

walk outside in the rain to get in position to walk down the aisle. Friends brought large golfing umbrellas to save the day. We laughed as we walked backwards holding umbrellas over Amber to the front of the church. We did our best to keep her dress from getting wet and we succeeded. Amber had chosen to be married on my birthday, December 15, so the church was decorated as a winter wonderland. Amber was lovely and her face was beaming with love.

Just before Amber was to walk down the aisle, a person came up to her and said hurtful words. She had done the same to me years earlier. I had warned Amber it would happen, it did, and we thought it was so funny. Thankfully, we didn't laugh out loud.

As the photographers were taking pictures after the ceremony, a candle fell onto Amber's dress, spilling wax across the train. The photographer later told me that Amber laughed and said, "Oh well, at least the wedding is over."

At the reception, someone forgot to play the music and we pretended there was no music planned. Someone else complained that they didn't like the food. Maybe the food wasn't their favorite things. The food served at Amber's wedding was her favorite dishes, made by her mother that loved her, and that mattered. Did I have the time to do it? No, but my child wanted her favorite things so that is what I did. My family helped. It was a success.

Amber told me that her wedding was exactly how she had always wanted it. She was lovely and happy the entire day. It was another "Oh Happy Day" in our lives. I am so proud we lived this day much like we lived all the others. We did the best we could and had a wonderful day filled with precious memories.

Amber and I were a team, and we faced the world together. Many times, we lived quietly through a difficult day, standing strong together with no tears shed as we quietly held hands. Holding hands for strength and encouragement worked for us. We shared the belief of being loyal to family and friends, and we defended them as needed. She and I shared secrets. It would be a tidbit of information, usually something funny, and we would retell the story and laugh until we could hardly breathe and our sides would hurt. That's what love is all about.

Amber grew up dressing cowgirl, preppy, glamorous, or casual and could confidently move between different social settings. When she was a teen, she worked. She wrote in her journal, "I started work at the radio station KDQN in De Queen. On my first day at work, the manager handed me a weather sheet and said, 'Practice because you are going on the air in five minutes.' Talk about pressure, but I made it and really loved working at the station."

Somehow within that five-minute period, Amber prepared herself to go live on the air and called me so I could listen. She spoke with a professional, clear voice. I was so proud of her. We celebrated that day. Later, Amber wrote how lucky she was to be working for KDQN and getting paid to have fun. Hearing my child's sweet, clear voice coming through the airwaves was pure joy. On that first day, I prayed so hard that she would be successful. She was and she loved it. I was thinking she is one brave kid!

I can't remember Amber ever going through the terrible twos or being a terrible teen. Once as a teen, though, she did worry me beyond understanding on a Saturday night. It was her first night staying out until 10:30 p.m. at the local game room. This was the cool hang-out spot for the kids of Wickes, and she was so excited to be going by herself.

I fell asleep and woke up after 11:00 p.m. Amber still wasn't home. My child, the one who always called when she was going to be a minute late, was late. But no call had come. She would have had to cross two railroad tracks to get home, and my imagination went wild. I started driving to town and met her about a block from the house. We returned home, and Amber calmly explained she wasn't even late. She said, "This is the night we turn the clocks back an hour, so I'm actually early." That possibly made sense to Amber and her friends but it hadn't helped me out at all. It was not funny that night but later this daylight-savings-time memory became one of those stories we would bring up and laugh hysterically about in the years ahead.

Amber may have been the only person who enjoyed hearing me sing. One day, someone criticized my singing voice, which made Amber furious. She told me they didn't know what they were talking about and would not accept their words. She wanted to sing with me and to have fun. She could not care less about someone else judging us. So we got out the karaoke machine and sang like we were pros. Her ears enjoyed the sound of my voice because of her love for me. And I loved that.

When we would go to Florida we would take Amber to a bowling alley where they played karaoke music and people would get up and sing. Amber would pick her songs and sing with her lovely voice. She was not afraid at all. One night when we were there three guys came and sat at our table. They said they were

Wingnut, Lugnut, and some other nut I can't remember. They were having a good time. They didn't bother us at all; they were just funny. They would compliment Amber's singing and encourage her forward. Merle was with us for protection of course. We all laughed about this night for years. Merle was definitely included in many of our laugh out loud moments.

One afternoon, Amber called me at work to say a boy from a nearby school had lost his date for the prom that night. She was heartbroken for the young man. I told her not to worry and to call the boy up and tell him she would go with him. I left work to curl her hair and help her get ready. She already had a dress we had bought for another prom.

The boy and his mother were so relieved. By the time he came to pick her up, she was transformed into a beautiful young woman, beaming with anticipation. I was so proud of her for taking action to transform a sad day for another into a special occasion. Amber had brightened up his day. She also brightened up her own day on purpose and I'm sure she had one grand time at that prom.

Amber was a little entertainer in our family. She participated in singing, acting, playing the piano, basketball, swimming, square dancing, clogging, and cheering. She was a good listener, empathetic to the concerns of others, and had a host of friends. Amber loved to talk on the telephone, confidently spoke her mind, and quickly adapted to change. She lived in the moment. She was highly intuitive, which allowed her to see people's motives much better than me. She was passionate about the humane treatment of animals and had planned a career in teaching primary-age children, for which her personality would have been a perfect match. Parents would have felt safe leaving their little ones in her care. Amber was the one person I could call on at the last minute for help. She was smart. I could trust her. My brave little golden child named Amber. I miss all these things about her.

In college, Amber had to write about her life and why she wanted to become a teacher. This is what she wrote in the assignment:

> My greatest accomplishment to date would have to be that I actually graduated from high school. In the beginning of the seventh grade, I became very sick. For the next six years, I was in and out of Baylor Medical Center in Dallas many times. My mom always stayed with me while I was in the hospital. We did my schoolwork the best we could. She was my teacher, best friend, mother, and playmate all at the same time. We made it through some tough times. We cried lots of tears, but we also had some fun times and actually looked for funny things throughout the days. One thing that I learned during this time is that some teachers, principals, and superintendents can look at students as individuals and realize we can't all fit into one perfect little mold. Many different individuals helped me along the way, and hopefully, I can repay them by helping some other student in need in the years to come.
>
> The greatest lesson that I feel I've learned is to live one day at a time and to care more about people than about things. I hope to be a teacher that teaches and also one that helps each child feel good about who they are.

This past year, the song "You'll Be There" by George Strait appeared in my iTunes account. Amber and I went to every George Strait concert that we could. We loved his movie *Pure Country*, which was filmed when Amber was in Baylor Hospital in Dallas. I believe some of the concert scenes in that movie were taped in Dallas and that people were allowed inside for free to be part of the crowd. Amber and I so wanted to go, but we had to wait to enjoy the movie and songs when they came out publicly.

Since Amber ascended to heaven, I have not listened to George Strait or watched *Pure Country*, as this was our favorite thing that we shared together. How did the song "You'll Be There" get into my iTunes? I had not heard of the song before. The words of the song talk about one living on earth as someone they love lives in heaven. The song came to me in some unusual way. I love it, and I thank God I have it, as I now have a George Strait song I can listen to. I can only agree with the words I've heard from the past, that God works in mysterious ways.

I loved Amber with my entire heart. There was no holding back. I loved her in all situations. She never had to act in a certain way for me to love her. This gave her confidence as she lived in the world. I loved her entirely, and she loved me right back. No one came between us. Others came into our lives, and we loved them. They moved into our circle and were loved by both of us, but they did not stand between Amber and me. My purpose was to have a child, love her every minute, have a joyful life, and love God. And we did that. Thank God we did, for now I know our love lives on forever, and that we will be back in each other's arms.

Though Amber now lives in heaven, she is continuing to affect people here on earth. If love is how we experience heaven on earth, Amber surely gave my life this most lovely of gifts.

19

♪♪ I Will Rise ♪♪

For I am persuaded, that neither death, nor life, nor angels, nor principalities, nor powers, nor things present, nor things to come, Nor height, nor depth, nor any other creature, shall be able to separate us from the love of God, which is in Christ Jesus our Lord.

—Romans 8:38-39 KJV

One of the first mornings after Amber left, I awoke holding her hand. My hand was between the mattress and the wall so I could not see it, but as her mother, I know Amber's hand. On that day, God allowed Amber and me to hold hands again. A precious gift was sent from heaven.

In January 2012, as I was walking through my bedroom, I heard Amber say, "Mom," as plain and clear as if she were standing beside me. My heart had been so saddened when she went to heaven that I would never be called mom or mother again on earth. But I was wrong because on that day, four years later, Amber called me mom. This lovely name was not taken from me on November 11, 2007.

God has allowed me to touch, see, and hear Amber from heaven. They were brief encounters but very real. When I rise to meet her, we will know and hold each other, talk together, and worship God throughout eternity. Thank God for this perfect miracle sent to a mother who loves her daughter completely and continues to miss her each day.

We learn about the normal order of death when facing the loss of our grandparents and then our aunts, uncles, and parents. Our children bury us, which is the normal and expected way. It doesn't take into account the untimely death of a child whom a parent must bury. The loss of a child is out of order for families and is such a tragedy that it has not been given a name in our language. But if it had been named, there would be no definition because it results in hearts being shattered beyond comprehension.

What happened will not magically become okay. Amber faced physical death before me, and her lovely spirit has gone to heaven. I know where she is. She is not lost. This knowledge is a tremendous blessing, but the separation is heartrending.

For a long time, the normal greetings my friends and I gave each other seemed like a lie if I responded in a positive way. Over time, I started saying that I was good. It worked, sounded normal to the other person, and was honest. I was as good as I could be. Life always has trials and worries. I've learned over time that when troubles come to try to look up and over them and move toward Christ. I have not perfected this plan, but I'm getting better.

The grace God sent from heaven on the day Amber left was enough to sustain me in my greatest hours of need. It was also a most wonderful gift for my future. We will be separated from loved ones here on earth, so tears will fall and hearts will grieve. To grieve means that we loved another person deeply. My heart aches for others when I know they are facing the physical death of a loved one, and I want them to know physical death is not the end of life. It can be the great beginning of eternal life in heaven for those who accept Jesus Christ as their Savior.

Over time, the full knowledge of Amber being with God has brought peace to me along with the assurance that we will be reunited for eternity. God's grace eased my spirit upward to heaven so I could survive the complete shattering of my heart. He has always been with me and has never left me alone.

My life on earth will not be the one I had pictured in my mind. God has freely given me glimpses into the heavenlies while still in my physical body. I don't know why or how He did this, but He did. I live with a great blessing, knowing beyond doubt that Amber lives with God in heaven. I cannot imagine how a parent faces the loss of a child without knowing he or she went to God in heaven.

My family and friends pulled or pushed me through the toughest of days. They helped me see a new vision of life on earth with Amber living in heaven. Friends are so important when tragedy strikes because they are not suffering the extreme grief of the family. Amber was protected and loved deeply by my family. We suffered the loss together as a strong family should when finding themselves in the center of a great loss. We recognize that the heartache cannot be fixed. Our family includes a host of faithful Christians who know that we will see Amber again in heaven.

The gifts that God gave me provided the courage to reach out to others who are struggling in a time of crisis. When I feel God wants me to go to someone in a time of need, I doubt my skills to help. But I am learning that if God chose me for the work, He will also provide the power and strength needed for the task. Usually, this work has been for one I did not know before. I pray during these times that I have brought some glimmer of hope or peace to someone's heart.

I want to become all God wants me to be. I commit myself to God's work and contribute all my good works in the memory of Amber as though she had done them. My work is her work if she lived on earth today. Our destiny remains as one. Our citizenship is set in heaven, and she went before me. When God calls me, I will leave this physical body behind and "I Will Rise" to meet Him and Amber in the sky. God has sent a beacon to mark the pathway to my heavenly home. My heart is set on going where I will live for eternity with God, the saints, the holy angels, and my precious Amber.

"Love Rising"

I closed my eyes and prayed to God how I could live when all was lost.
In the stillness of the air, He was present, filled with care.
He sent His angels in amber light that caught my heart and held it tight.
They had been watching with hearts of gold,
The angels cried as they took her home.
He knew I'd miss her with every breath and shed the veil with His amazing grace.
She went to heaven on that day and lives with angels in the golden rays.
Today I love Him, I love Him more; He has my child beyond heaven's door.
He will call me where angels dwell, my child will greet me; know all is well.

—p. dickerson

20

♪♪ Jesus Messiah ♪♪

In the beginning God created the heaven and the earth.
So God created man in his own image, in the image
of God created he him; male and female created he
them.

(Genesis 1:1, 27 KJV)

This people have I formed for myself; they shall shew
forth my praise.

(Isaiah 43:21 KJV)

God is the one true God. God is love and more powerful than all other spirits, people, or things the human race worships. God exists in the Holy Trinity as three divine persons: the Father, the Son Jesus Christ, and the Holy Spirit. They are unique but one, equal to each other, existing in total unity. They are God in three persons with distinct relations only to each other. God created heaven and earth, and He is the God who loves and demonstrates grace to us. No person or nation should underestimate the power of the Holy Trinity actively participating in perfect harmony in all things of heaven and earth.

God sent His Son to live on earth. Following are the factual events surrounding the life of "Jesus Messiah". Each event is recorded clearly in the Bible. For this section, I rely heavily on God's Word, the Bible:

> And in the sixth month the angel Gabriel was sent from God unto a city of Galilee, named Nazareth, To a virgin espoused to a man whose name was Joseph, of the house of David; and the virgin's name was Mary. And the angel came in unto her, and said, Hail, thou that art highly favoured, the Lord is with thee: blessed art thou among women. And when she saw him, she was troubled at his saying, and cast in her mind what manner of salutation this should be. And the angel said unto her, Fear not, Mary: for thou hast found favour with God. And, behold, thou shalt conceive in thy womb, and bring forth a son, and shalt call his name JESUS. He shall be great, and shall be called the Son of the Highest: and the Lord God shall give unto him the throne of his father David: And he shall reign over the house of Jacob for ever; and of his kingdom there shall be no end. Then said Mary unto the angel, How shall this be, seeing I know not a man? And the angel answered and said unto her, The Holy Ghost shall come upon thee, and the power of the Highest shall overshadow thee: therefore also that holy thing which shall be born of thee shall be called the Son of God. And, behold, thy cousin Elisabeth, she hath also conceived a son in her old age: and this is the sixth month with her, who was called barren. (Luke 1:26-36 KJV)

> Now the birth of Jesus Christ was on this wise: When as his mother Mary was espoused to Joseph, before they came together, she was found with child of the Holy

Ghost. Then Joseph her husband, being a just man, and not willing to make her a public example, was minded to put her away privily. But while he thought on these things, behold, the angel of the LORD appeared unto him in a dream, saying, Joseph, thou son of David, fear not to take unto thee Mary thy wife: for that which is conceived in her is of the Holy Ghost. And she shall bring forth a son, and thou shalt call his name JESUS: for he shall save his people from their sins. Now all this was done, that it might be fulfilled which was spoken of the Lord by the prophet, saying, Behold, a virgin shall be with child, and shall bring forth a son, and they shall call his name Emmanuel, which being interpreted is, God with us. Then Joseph being raised from sleep did as the angel of the Lord had bidden him, and took unto him his wife: And knew her not till she had brought forth her firstborn son: and he called his name JESUS. (Matthew 1:18-25 KJV)

And it came to pass in those days, that there went out a decree from Caesar Augustus that all the world should be taxed. And all went to be taxed, every one into his own city. And Joseph also went up from Galilee, out of the city of Nazareth, into Judaea, unto the city of David, which is called Bethlehem; (because he was of the house and lineage of David) To be taxed with Mary his espoused wife, being great with child. And so it was, that, while they were there, the days were accomplished that she should be delivered. And she brought forth her firstborn son, and wrapped him in swaddling clothes, and laid him in a manger; because there was no room for them in the inn. And there were in the same country shepherds abiding in the field, keeping watch over their flock by night. And, lo, the angel of the Lord came upon them, and the glory of the Lord shone round about them: and they were sore afraid. And the angel said unto them, Fear not:

for, behold, I bring you good tidings of great joy, which shall be to all people. For unto you is born this day in the city of David a Saviour, which is Christ the Lord. And this shall be a sign unto you; Ye shall find the babe wrapped in swaddling clothes, lying in a manger. And suddenly there was with the angel a multitude of the heavenly host praising God, and saying, Glory to God in the highest, and on earth peace, good will toward men. And it came to pass, as the angels were gone away from them into heaven, the shepherds said one to another, Let us now go even unto Bethlehem, and see this thing which is come to pass, which the Lord hath made known unto us. And they came with haste, and found Mary, and Joseph, and the babe lying in a manger. And when they had seen it, they made known abroad the saying which was told them concerning this child. And all they that heard it wondered at those things which were told them by the shepherds. But Mary kept all these things, and pondered them in her heart. And the shepherds returned, glorifying and praising God for all the things that they had heard and seen, as it was told unto them. (Luke 2:1, 3-20 JKV)

God sent His Son, Jesus Christ, to live on earth in human form. Jesus came to earth, taught God's ways, and committed no sin. He shed His blood on the cross and died for our sins. God loves us so much that He allowed His own Son to suffer and die for our sins. We didn't deserve it, nor did we earn it. God's mercy through this act gave us the opportunity to be saved by grace to live eternal life in heaven.

God created you to worship Him. You are a unique person with special gifts given to you by God. Every person other than Christ has sinned. But God still loves all people and wants them to love Him and inherit everlasting life in heaven. You have the opportunity to choose to love God and live for Him the remainder of your life.

> Even the righteousness of God which is by faith of Jesus Christ unto all and upon all them that believe: for there is no difference: (Romans 3:22 KJV)

> For by grace are ye saved through faith; and that not of yourselves: it is the gift of God: Not of works, lest any man should boast. (Ephesians 2:8-9 KJV)

Today the choice is yours, and your answer is critical for your eternal life. If you are ready to follow Jesus, acknowledge before others that you:

1. Declare yourself a sinner;
2. Turn from sin and toward God;
3. Confess your belief in the Lord Jesus Christ, that He died for your sins, and that God, His Father, raised Him from the dead;
4. Ask Jesus Christ to come into your heart and allow the Holy Spirit to direct your life;
5. Thank God for the forgiveness of your sins, the gift of salvation, and for everlasting life; and
6. Be baptized in the name of the Lord. (Acts 10: 48 KJV)

> That if thou shalt confess with thy mouth the Lord Jesus, and shalt believe in thine heart that God hath raised him from the dead, thou shalt be saved. For with the heart man believeth unto righteousness; and with the mouth confession is made unto salvation. For the scripture saith, Whosoever believeth on him shall not be ashamed. For there is no difference between the Jew and the Greek: for

the same Lord over all is rich unto all that call upon him. For whosoever shall call upon the name of the Lord shall be saved. (Romans 10:9-13 KJV)

Each person will make the choice that determines where they spend eternity. A 2005 Harris poll revealed 82 percent of Americans believe in God, 70 percent in life after death, and six out of ten in the existence of heaven and hell.

Jennifer Harper, "Majority in U.S. Believe in God," in the Washington Times (25 December 2005).

A great number of Americans believe that God exists, that individuals exist after death, and that heaven and hell are real. The clock ticks forward in time, and with every second, we grow closer to the moment when our heart will beat no more. I pray that before you die a physical death you will ask God into your heart so you will live throughout eternity in heaven where the saints and angels dwell.

21

♪♪ Be Still ♪♪

Be still, and know that I am God: I will be exalted among
the heathen, I will be exalted in the earth.

—Psalm 46:10 KJV

"Pure silence," I heard in my spirit. God wanted me to
spend time in silence away from all interruptions,
obligations, and noise. I needed to learn how to calm
my heart and mind, as I must "Be Still" in this secret place where I
can silently worship in God's imminent presence.

The more silent my heart, mind, and soul become, the closer
He comes, fills the silent space with His Holy Spirit, and we
speak heart to heart. He restores my heart, mind, and soul and
gives me strength. Time no longer has meaning. Since finding
this most secret place, I can no longer imagine life without it.
My heart's desire is to return there. I am striving to learn how
to dwell in the secret place regardless of where I am or what is
going on around me. To do this will require another level of faith,
so it has become a new personal goal. He that dwelleth in the

secret place of the most High shall abide under the shadow of the Almighty. (Psalm 91:1 KJV)

The meaning of prayer is to communicate with God with a sincere heart, seeking His will for your life. Sincerity draws Him closer to the secret place where communication freely flows. Pray to see Him, hear Him, and to know Him more each day.

"Be Still" of heart and know that He is always with you. God is not silent to those who seek Him. He knows your concerns before you tell Him. When you reach that precious place where your heart, mind, and soul strive to hear Him, you will. To pray one is asking for supernatural intervention from God. It is hard for me to imagine a person who has not faced a need to pray.

> And ye shall seek me, and find me, when ye shall search for me with all your heart. (Jeremiah 29:13 KJV)

> After this manner therefore pray ye: Our Father which art in heaven, Hallowed be thy name. Thy kingdom come, Thy will be done on earth, as it is in heaven. Give us this day our daily bread. And forgive us our debts, as we forgive our debtors. And lead us not into temptation, but deliver us from evil: For thine is the kingdom, and the power, and the glory, forever. Amen. (Matthew 6:9-13 KJV)

This is known as the Lord's Prayer. Many times, I have repeated the Lord's Prayer printed in the King James Version of the Bible. It is the one written on my heart from childhood and seems to be perfect for all time. I doubted that I knew how to pray for Amber when she was critically ill. Today, I know and accept that if I made a mistake in my wording, the Holy Spirit intervened on my behalf.

The following Bible verse taught me I held no burden of guilt that I did not pray well enough for my child. Likewise the Spirit also helpeth our infirmities: for we know not what we should pray for as we ought: but the Spirit itself maketh intercession for us with groanings which cannot be uttered. (Romans 8:26 KJV)

22

♪♪ Holy Spirit Rain Down ♪♪

Nevertheless I tell you the truth; It is expedient for you
that I go away: for if I go not away, the Comforter will
not come unto you; but if I depart, I will send him unto
you. And when he is come, he will reprove the world of
sin, and of righteousness, and of judgment:

—John 16:7-8 KJV

The Advocate of which Jesus spoke was the Holy Spirit.
The Holy Spirit can open the eyes of your heart to know
God in a way that you did not know Him before. It is not
possible to pray heartfelt prayers, the kind that God desires, without
the Holy Spirit. To pray is asking for supernatural power to reign
over earthly events.

To accept the reality of the Holy Spirit, we must come to the
conclusion that there is another world that we cannot see. The natural
dwelling place of the Holy Spirit is the heart, which is where pure
worship can be given to God. When others see evidence of the
supernatural gifts given to another, they will desire to know more,

which may lead them straight to God, Jesus, and the Holy Spirit. Christians who allow the Holy Spirit to dwell in their hearts will produce the fruit of the Spirit for all to see. But the fruit of the Spirit is love, joy, peace, longsuffering, gentleness, goodness, faith, meekness, temperance: against such there is no law. (Galatians 5:22-23 KJV).

Ask the Holy Spirit to dwell within you. Knowing that the Holy Spirit is present and guiding you physically, emotionally, and verbally will allow you to walk forth with strength, power, and assurance. Extraordinary events can unfold when you walk within the power of the Holy Spirit. There is no place this side of heaven more joyous than when you experience the overwhelming sensation of being in His presence.

It is important to understand messages brought by the Holy Spirit. You must refer each vision, dream, or statement to the Bible for clarification. Supernatural experiences are subject to the authority of the Bible. If the message disagrees with the Bible, you either have not understood it correctly or it did not come from God.

When we sing "Holy Spirit Rain Down" at Heritage Church in Van Buren, it actually feels like the Holy Spirit is pouring across the people. His showing up in such a mighty way, changing the course of people's lives, is a great blessing. I thank God that I attend a church where the pastor and the members believe the Holy Spirit is with us each week.

> For as many as are led by the Spirit of God, they are the sons of God. For ye have not received the spirit of bondage again to fear; but ye have received the Spirit of adoption, whereby we cry, Abba, Father. The Spirit itself beareth witness with our spirit, that we are the children of God: (Romans 8:14-16 KJV)

23

♪♪ While We Were Sleeping ♪♪

America is a large, powerful country made up of people who came from all over the earth. We all look the way God intended us. If we stand up together, united as the Christian Nation with firm determination, we can change the face of this country. We must lay aside the issues of doctrine, denomination, and political party and stand together in unity of the Christian faith. Neither Jesus nor the disciples taught us to divide ourselves into smaller groups. If we unite, God will guide us forward, and together we will far exceed the expectations of people and other nations, as we will have the power of God with us. His is the power that can change the world.

America has been falling "While We Were Sleeping." We the people missed seeing our country turn away from God. The fall is catching speed, and only a great save by the Christian people will turn this country around and back to God. Our country must quickly return as the greatest nation on earth. We must stand strong with Israel. God told us to do this. He did not say only if it was convenient. He said to do it. I believe America will stand with Israel or it will continue to fall. The Christian people must guide this nation in every way. Time is short, and work is necessary. It is our responsibility to ensure that our leaders are trustworthy and courageously set in place to unite and protect all the people of our land.

We are possibly at the beginning of the fourth Great Awakening when great numbers of the population will come to know God by heart. Enlightened Christians will stand up for the church to become a true place of worship, and its members will walk as missionaries across the land doing God's work. Great men and women will rise up to make immense changes from this awakening with God and His Word guiding them. We must not waste time listening to lies, nor sit idle and allow others to take away our rights as citizens of the United States of America. We have a voice. God does not want us to be silent. We must stand up and say what He is asking us to say.

Our combined Christian voices can prepare the people of America for the second coming of Jesus Christ. If we are with God, nothing can stop a great revival in America that will bring the Holy Spirit and His mighty power. We must pray without ceasing for this great awakening to come now. We must set our spirits free across this land to tell the people how to become saved by the grace of God. Hearts set afire with a burning desire to know God will lead many others to know Him. I live in great anticipation for God's people to unite and the miraculous things that will follow.

> But this is that which was spoken by the prophet Joel;
> And it shall come to pass in the last days, saith God, I
> will pour out of my Spirit upon all flesh: and your sons
> and your daughters shall prophesy, and your young men
> shall see visions, and your old men shall dream dreams:

And on my servants and on my handmaidens I will pour
out in those days of my Spirit; and they shall prophesy:
(Acts 2:16-18 KJV)

Battle Cry

We are God's holy army, forged together by our faith.
We joined before His witness, now time is running late.
God our Chief Commander has given out the charge.
The battle looms before us, the battle will be large.

The Bible warned its coming, spreading across
the land.
Will we rise with Israel, or sink in sifting sand?
God said ignore false prophets, their words
will not withstand.
Deceit is their sole purpose, lies used as sword
in hand.

God forewarned of His coming,
in crisis we now stand.
Send out the cry to others, save many by His plan.
Our God will soon be coming,
glory filling all the air.
Angels and saints will join Him,
the Bible did forebear.

Our voices must not be silent.
Our hands must not be bound.
Our eyes will see His coming.
Our ears perceive the sound.
Our God provides protection.
Our hearts lie in His hands.

paula dickerson

24

♪♪ Knowing You'll Be There ♪♪

If ye then be risen with Christ, seek those things which
are above, where Christ sitteth on the right hand of God.
Set your affection on things above, not on things on the
earth.

—Colossians 3:1-2 KJV

D r. Raymond Moody wrote, "A number of studies . . .
have established that a high percentage of bereaved
persons have visions of the deceased. For instance,
as many as 75% of parents who lose a child to death will have
some kind of apparition of that child within a year of the loss. The
experience is a relief for most of the parents and will greatly reduce
their grief." Moody concluded that such visions are comforting
because they provide us with another reason to trust that our loved
ones are not "gone" but still survive and thrive in an afterlife.

After many months of research and countless hours of listening
to people tell their near-death stories, Dr. Raymond Moody put it
this way:

I am left, not with conclusions or evidence or proofs, but with something much less definite—feelings, questions, analogies, puzzling facts to be explained. In fact, it might be more appropriate to ask, not what conclusions I have drawn on the basis of my study, but rather how the study has affected me personally. In response I can only say: There is something very persuasive about seeing a person describe his experience which cannot easily be conveyed in writing. Their near-death experiences were very real events to these people, and through my association with them, the experiences have become real events to me.[2]

And he said, While the child was yet alive, I fasted and wept: for I said, Who can tell whether GOD will be gracious to me, that the child may live? But now he is dead, wherefore should I fast? can I bring him back again? I shall go to him, but he shall not return to me. (2 Samuel 12:22-23 KJV)

I do not know how I would have survived if God had not sent the remarkable gifts from heaven shared in "Glory Came in Amber Rays." Why God chose to send them to me, I cannot explain, but I accept them as being real as any other happening in my world and understand that they are above the natural. I believe God's heaven is close to us each day, and when He decides, a person can see into the heavenlies.

God has allowed me to know Amber lives in heaven. I have no need to worry about her because God and the angels are caring for her. But I miss her more than I could ever explain. Amber will be waiting for me when I rise to heaven. The words from the hymn

---

[2]   James L. Garlow and Keith Wall, *Heaven and the Afterlife* (Minneapolis, Minnesota; Bethany House, 2009), 21, 30.

"Knowing You'll Be There" makes it easy to go home, describe exactly how I feel. When I take that mighty step someday and rise into the heavens, I'll be with my child again glowing in amber rays."

Amber is alive and shines as sunlight. She will not come to me. I will go to her.

25

♪♪ My Girl ♪♪

Amber was and always will be "My Girl." I had the ringtone on my cell phone set to "My Girl" when she called. Hearing the tune made my heart happy on a normal day. It is difficult to explain what a loss this one little thing is. Amber always recorded my voicemail message on my phone. When I'd get a new phone, she would record a new message. I removed her voice after she went to heaven for Brentley because I imagined it could be confusing to him to hear her answer my phone Brentley knew his mother had gone to heaven.

Amber and Brentley lived on the farm where Amber grew up. Sometimes Amber would drive cattle to the sale barn and Brentley would go with her riding in his little car seat. He was a true cowboy and dressed in western clothes just like his mother. A man at the sale barn became upset with his mother. I can't remember why the man became upset but I remember well Brentley telling me about it. He did not like someone being mean to his "Meme". He was totally prepared to fight the man if he had moved toward his mother. There would have been no holding back. He was serious and determined. She was and always will be his "Meme".

Amber was such a good and loving child. She wrote the following, which she posted on her MySpace page on July 11, 2007, where it remains today. When I read this poem I was thinking, that is "My Girl", she wrote those words for all the world to see. The last line she typed in red telling us she loved God completely. What a blessing to a mother's heart.

Current mood: grateful

Some of the things that I enjoy in life . . .
(just to name a few)
I love the smell of fresh cut hay . . .
I love the smell of rain . . .
I love the smell of a river . . .
I love the smell of a horse . . .
I love holding my baby boy . . .
I love spending time with my husband . . .
I love spending time with my family and friends . . .
I love it when a hot cowboy tips his hat at ya and gives
you a grin . . .
I love riding horses . . .
I love working with cows . . .
I love to read the newspaper . . .
I love to talk on the phone . . .
I love to shop for shoes . . .
I love the sound of the ocean . . .
I love the fact that I feel loved and always have felt
that way . . .
I love knowing who my friends are and that they are
always there for me . . .
I love feeling healthy . . .
I love being honest . . .
***I love God and thank him for all that I have
been blessed with!!!!!!!!!!!!***

26

♪♪ In My Daughter's Eyes ♪♪

A love letter to me:

Dearest Mom,

Hi! How are you doing? I am fine just had some time and I wanted to write and say Thank you for all of the wonderful things you do and have done for me. I could not have asked for a better mother. We look alike, act alike, and talk alike . . . And I am very proud to be like you!

I hope you have a wonderful holiday and that Santa is good to you. Please just relax and take it easy over Christmas—you need a break!!

Well I better go for now. Thank you for always making my Christmas special and wonderful. Most of all . . . Thanks for being my Mom!

Love always and forever!

Amber CarLeigh

A mber's words are so dear to my heart. I don't have to wonder if she loved me or if she enjoyed being like me. She said she did. I love that. Because of this true love, everything else, including doubts, fade into the background

One day, I drove to Wickes to visit with Amber and Brentley. She was so excited about a new song. She and Brentley met me at the car with a CD, and we listened to the song "In My Daughter's Eyes" two or three times. What a special moment in our lives. She was saying, "These are the words, this is how I feel." I will never forget that day and the love shining in her eyes. The song tells of a beautiful relationship between a mother and a daughter. My favorite words in the lovely song by Martina McBride are:

> This miracle God gave to me, gives me strength when
> I am weak,
> The truth is plain to see, she was sent to rescue me,
> I find reason to believe, in my daughter's eyes.

When God sent Amber to me it changed everything about my life. When people speak of her now they always mention her lovely smile, her knowing how to laugh out loud, and her kindness to people.

Amber and I knew how to love and when little Brentley came he was right there in the middle, loved completely. Brentley brought joy and happiness into her life. She was protective of him and did everything possible to ensure he was a healthy, happy little boy. Brentley was like a little athlete as a baby and he would fly around the rooms jumping on and over the furniture. Amber calmly took it all in stride. She was determined to raise Brentley her way. My heart is thankful I have a daughter who became a lovely mother.

A love letter to Amber: March 11, 2012

Dear Amber CarLeigh,

This is the day you turn thirty-four. What joy was in my heart the moment the doctor first placed you in my arms. I have loved you from the first moment I knew you were to be. I will do everything I can to ensure Brentley has a wonderful life and grows up to be happy like you. I will help him remember you, teach him how much you love him, and I will encourage him to love God.

I dedicate the remainder of my life on earth to God in your memory. The good things I do for Him will be as though you did them. I pray for peace, grace, strength, and rest for the days ahead and for knowledge to know what God has left for me to do on earth.

In awhile, we will be reunited when God calls my name. My free spirit will strive to live in the space between heaven and earth as often as possible each day and night. I know this is the space where you and I speak, heart to heart. There will be no moment throughout eternity of which I do not love you completely by heart, mind, and soul.

With love forever and ever,

Mom

27

♪♪ Blessed Assurance ♪♪

I gathered all my courage and started submitting "Glory Came in Amber Rays" to different publishing companies. Each company asks for information in a different form so to submit a manuscript once takes a while. The first night I probably submitted it to four or five companies. The next day I set a goal to submit the manuscript once a day.

I am a first time author with little understanding of the publishing world. I didn't know the next steps to publication. Companies called and sent email messages. Mark VanDemon, a representative from Crossbooks, called. He told me if they were to publish the manuscript it would go through the theological review process first. He was the first and only person in the publishing world to mention a theological review to me and I knew in my heart it was right. It immediately separated Crossbooks from all other publishers. I have no desire to publish writing that is in disagreement with the Bible. If Crossbooks could assure me that I had not written in disagreement with the Bible, they were the needed company to publish the book.

I had asked a good friend and member of Heritage Church, Gary Nishmuta, to review the book in the same manner before I submitted the book to publishing companies. We were all on the same page. Thank God I was surrounded by others that could review "Glory Came in Amber Rays."

I submitted the manuscript to Crossbooks and I waited. I was notified when the book was sent to Nashville, Tennessee for the theological review. I waited. Christmas came and went and I'd heard nothing about the book. I started imagining for the first time Crossbooks would make a decision to not publish "Glory Came in Amber Rays." I began to doubt myself. Was I doing the will of God by sharing the story?

Suddenly I was awakened by the music box of the little girl at the piano playing. The song was "The Entertainer". I had been asleep in the next room. I sat up and listened as the music box played the song once and then played it again a little softer. I didn't get up until the music box stopped playing. I walked to the sunroom and stood in amazement that the music box had played by itself for a second time. Amber's music box collection sits behind a glass door in a tall white cabinet in the sunroom.

Suddenly the little porcelain clown music box sitting on the shelf above the little girl played four distinct notes. The clown music box was Amber's first music box. I purchased it when Amber was little and in Baylor Hospital in Dallas because she was very sick. I would play the music box when she had to have a shot, have blood drawn, or to just brighten the day. Amber and I would focus on the beautiful little clown as she played "Be A Clown" and she swayed to the music. I would whisper sweet nothings in Amber's ear and hold her tight until things were better. We made it through sad, scary moments with the help of a little clown.

The baby grand piano Amber and I played together sits to the left of the music box cabinet. I had completely closed the piano for Christmas so I could place my Santa collection on its top. The keyboard was also closed with a picture of the words describing love from 1 Corinthians 13:4-8 sitting on its lid. Unexpectedly the piano played one note. Just one precious note played clearly in the air.

On this day, January 9, 2013, three different musical instruments had played alone one after the other. As I was still standing just looking at the music boxes a little white wisp of a shadow passed me on the right and vanished into the wall. I can't tell you how it happened. I can only say, "Hallelujah, what a wonderful blessing." I had held a belief that as I improved, and God knew I would survive with Amber in heaven, the gifts would stop flowing down to me. I had been wrong. Because He loves me, God sent a remarkable gift. Thank God for wonderful gifts. On this day I felt as though I had received the "Blessed Assurance" from God that He continued to watch over me and that I had not disappointed Him by writing or submitting the book for publication.

The following day January 10, 2013, I received an email and a telephone call from Crossbooks telling me "Glory Came in Amber Rays" had passed the theological review process. This means a trained theologian had carefully read "Glory Came in Amber Rays" and they granted the work the Lifeway seal saying the book is written in accordance with the CrossBooks Statement of Faith.

Next I received a beautiful certificate from Crossbooks about "Glory Came in Amber Rays", my writing skills, and documentation stating the work met all the requirements of the theological review. What a lovely gift to receive in the mail. I didn't expect it but I'm so proud of it. I can imagine Amber being proud of me in heaven for this work. I can almost hear her saying, "I told you Mom, you could do it." My little Amber was sent to rescue me from an ordinary life.

28

♪♪ My Tribute ♪♪
To God Be the Glory

This book is written with love for God, in memory of my only child, Amber CarLeigh, and for her son Brentley. She came from heaven as the light of my life. She now lives in heaven with God and the angels in the rainbow colors of light. I thank God for allowing me to be Amber's mother. What a difference she has made in my life.

I am most grateful to my husband Merle Dickerson for his love and support throughout the years and especially during the time my world shattered apart when my precious Amber went to heaven. He held me when there was nothing more we could do and there were no words to be said. His strength and love for God helped guide us forward through days we did not understand.

I want my parents, John and Imogene Tidwell, who love each other well to know how much I love and thank them for raising me in a Christian home. I was taught that God was real and working in our world from the beginning, and I have no memory of not believing or trusting in God. Parents can give no greater gift to a child.

I have a loving sister, Patricia, and brother, Mitchell Tidwell, who I thank for all the wonderful, fun memories we made together as children and for standing beside me as I faced the greatest tragedy a mother can endure. Their loving spouses, children, and grandchildren surrounded me with love and care so I would not face this heartrending loss alone. They remain with me to this day.

I have a niece, Andi Davis, who grew up with Amber. Andi was seven months older, so she took the lead in many of their activities. Andi, Amber, and I did many things together. In every crisis I faced, Andi stood beside me. These were not easy times and our hearts were breaking, but Andi never wavered. I love her from the heart and pray she knows completely that she made a difference to Amber and to me.

Amber's close friend Amy Montgomery has told me that she felt Amber was asking her from heaven to make sure I was okay. Amy continues to call, text, and send me notes on Facebook. She writes lovely stories, telling of adventures she and Amber had in childhood. She and Amber looked so much alike when they were children that when I kissed the top of a head, I could not be sure which little girl I had kissed! Amy is now like a little angel unaware, bringing sunshine to my days for Amber. What a blessing she has been in my life.

I thank God for my precious friend Debbie Thomas. She came in as I was saying no and has stayed with me throughout this journey. Debbie stood strong and encouraged me to move forward each day.

Through my tears, I have seen tears falling from Debbie eyes as she would turn to leave me. That memory will forever be etched in my mind. What a strong and loving friend.

My pastor, Wes Hilliard, of Heritage Church listened to me as I shared pieces of the heavenly events and did not doubt my words for which I'm most grateful. He prayed with and for me and reassured me that God would stay with me. There were times when he said that this would take another level of faith, and he was right. Today I'm wondering, how many levels are there?

I feel blessed to have the opportunity to hear Wes preach each week. He preaches from the Bible and he actively teaches us about God. He taught me to pray for spiritual gifts, and I trusted him. I prayed the prayers while asking God to protect me from Satan. I have had three brief encounters with Satan, which were incredibly short but horrendous. I purposely chose to not include them in this book.

I feel as though God handpicked our closest neighbors, Torin Johnson and his wife Debbie. Their children, Tobin and Taryn, seem like our grandchildren, and we love them. We've been blessed as well by Torin's parents, Pastor Bobby and Pam Johnson. They happily share the grandchildren and have provided continuous support during these years of trial. Torin and Tobin watched over us on the normal days and came at critical times when we needed them the most. Torin serves as youth pastor at Van Buren First Assembly of God, so on this spiritual journey, his biblical knowledge and caring personality made the difference.

Pastor George Lynn from Living Word Church provided support and guidance on many occasions. Many times, he prayed beautiful prayers with Merle and me. His words were so very special and left me feeling that the Holy Spirit was with him. He knows the Bible well and guided me to Scriptures where I needed to focus my attention. I thank him greatly for each time he encouraged me to rely on God and believe I could live forward.

I am thankful to Dr. Jeff Hamby and Dr. Rocky Cullens who took time from their busy schedules and gifted me time to talk. They were kind and caring and encouraged me to trust myself and move forward cautiously. They always believed that I could live forward, although they knew I had to find my own pathway to a new life. This was critical during the time I felt it was impossible to go on living. I say thank you from my heart to two doctors who did far more than their training required.

I thank God for sending Christa Nishmuta to me with purity of heart and mind and with the desire to help a mother who no longer believed she was a mother. She brought joy back into our home and lives. Along with Christa came her parents Gary and Diane Nishmuta. They have been open in attempting to answer difficult questions on many topics. Their knowledge and mighty prayers have brought peace and understanding on many nights. Diane took this book and edited it over many hours. My heart and mind recognize how much she improved the book with each correction or suggestion. Gary reviewed the book and its content in relation to the Bible. Thank you does not seem appropriate for what they freely gave. I'm left searching for words to explain what they did for Amber and me. It is amazing that God sent a family that included an artist, a professional editor, and one who could perform theological review. What a blessing!

Those mentioned here are a few of the large group of family and friends who have supported me the last five years. They came and cared. They stood with me when there were no words to say. I love each person who came or sent cards and books with kindness in their hearts. I often cried my way through opening the mail, but I want everyone to know beyond doubt that the messages made a difference. They gave me strength to live long enough to see a glimpse of a life with joy though Amber and I are separated. At times, that space grows very small. Those are the moments I pray for.

Many I did not know offered kindness in ways I would not have imagined. Until this tragedy occurred in my life, I did not know how much I needed people and what a difference their words and deeds would mean. I believe God sent them to me. They were as angels unaware.

In addition to the Bible, I have read the works of A. W. Tozer, John Newton, William Wilberforce, Billy Graham, Don Piper, Gregg Laurie, and others. I know their words have influenced my mind and thinking, but their books brought me comfort, and I learned more about God through their writing. I am thankful they placed pen to paper and shared their love of God with others.

I want to encourage you to think about the things you worry about during any given day. Are they really that important? Imagine that today is the last day you talk to the ones you love deeply on earth. What would you want to make sure they know?

We take for granted that our loved ones will live a long life right up to that minute when they do not. Regrets will never change the "what" that happens, and you will live with what you said and did with them forever and ever. Have you told them out loud while looking them in the eye that you love them? The greatest thing you can do for your loved ones is to love them completely as God loves you.

Looking back on my life now, I see it was scattered with ordinary miracles. They came when least expected and remain a part of me. I hold those memories safe in my heart as little treasures. I will never be the person I was before Amber went to heaven. I had to learn things I did not want to know; but because God came to me, I have a future with Him.

Amber lives in precious memories to those who loved her. The grave did not hold her, and she lives in heaven with God and the angels. I pray that her friends and family see her again in the radiant colors of the rainbow. To do that, they will have made the personal choice to live for God. Amber would so want that for them.

Amber and I had a most private life. Because we had each other for support, we had no need to share a lot about our lives with other people. I am breaking our rule completely and sharing my most precious memories and spiritual happenings with you, the reader. I don't know how far this book will travel. But if it helps to bring salvation to one through Jesus Christ our Savior, it is worth it. I have literally laid it on the line, one word at a time. I pray it was God's will for me to do this work.

I plan to live the remainder of my days on earth for God. When He calls out my name, I plan to rise to heaven. My child will be there with many of my friends and relatives. It will be a wonderful reunion day. I am determined. I will not turn back. Heaven is my destiny.

This is "My Tribute—To God Be the Glory"!

Sources

Somewhere along the pathway, I started using song titles as chapter titles. Each of these songs has a special meaning in my life and seemed appropriate to the happening. I've learned through research many of the songs were written in response to a beautiful though sometimes tragic love story.

1. Gloria Estefan, vocal performance of "Music of My Heart," by Bob Seger and Alto Reed, recorded 1999, on Music of My Heart, Soundtrack from the Motion Picture, Sony Music Entertainment, Inc. Compact disk.

2. Susan Boyle, vocal performance of "I Dreamed a Dream," by Herb Hertzmer and Claude-Michael Schonberg, recorded 2009, on I Dreamed a Dream, Columbia Records Compact disk.

3. Aaliyah Joint, vocal performance of "Turn the Page," by Diane Warren and David Foster, recorded 1999 on Music of My Heart Soundtrack from the Motion Picture, Sony Music Entertainment Inc. Compact disk.

4. Sarah McLachlan, vocal performance of "Angel," by Sarah McLachlan, recorded 1997, on Surfacing, Wild Sky Studios. Compact disk.

5. Darlene Zschech, vocal performance of "Amazing Grace," by John Newton, recorded 2007 on Amazing Grace—Timeless Hymns of Faith, Integrity Media Inc. Compact disk.

6. Blake, Glenda, lyricist & composer, "In the Middle of the Night," 1990.

7. Alison Krauss, vocal performance of "When You Say Nothing at All," by Paul Overstreet and Don Schlitz recorded 2002 on Alison Krauss & Union Station: Live. Compact disk.

8. Celine Dion and Andrea Bocelli, vocal performance of "The Prayer," by Alberto Testa and Tony Renis, recorded 1998 on These Are Special Times, Music Entertainment. Compact disk.

9. Guy Penrod, vocal performance of "Knowing What I Know About Heaven," by Sarah Darling, Dave Robbins, and Billy Austen, recorded 2010 on Breathe Deep, Gaither Music Group/Servant Records. Compact disk.

10. Jewel Kilcher, vocal performance of "Somewhere Over the Rainbow", by Harold Arlen and Herbert Stothart, recorded 2009 on Lullaby, Harburg, E.Y., Summerset Entertainment. Compact disk.

11. Jewel Kilcher, vocal performance of "Face of Love", by Jewel Kilcher, recorded 1999 on Joy: A Holiday Collection, Atlantic Record Corporation. Compact disk.

12. Addison Road, vocal performance of "This Little Light of Mine," by Harvy Dixon Loes, recorded 2010 on This Little Light of Mine, Fair Trade Services, LLC. Compact disk.

13. Michael Nyman, piano solo performance, "The Scent of Love", by Michael Nyman, recorded 1993 on The Piano Original Music from the Film, Virgin Records, Ltd. Compact disk.

14. Nicole Sponberg, vocal performance of "Knowing You", by Graham Kendrick, recorded 2010 on On Our Way Home, Club Records, Inc. Compact disk.

15. Michael W. Smith, vocal performance of "Friends", by Deborah D. Smith and Michael W. Smith, recorded 1983 onMichael W Smith Project. Compact disk.

16. Jewel Kilcher, vocal performance of "Angel Standing By", by Jewel Kilcher, recorded 1994 on Pieces of You, Atlantic Recording Corp. Compact disk.

17. Selah, vocal performance of "My Jesus I Love Thee", by William Ralph Featherston and Adoniram Judson Gordon, recorded 2009 on You Deliver Me, Curb Record, Inc. Compact disk.

18. Van Morrison, vocal performance of "Brown Eyed Girl" by Van Morrison, recorded 1967 on Blowin' Your Mind! Bang Records. Compact disk.

19. Susan Boyle, vocal performance of "How Great Thou Art" Carl Gustav Boberg and Stuart K. Hine recorded 2009 on How Great Thou Art, Columbia Records. Compact disk.

20. Edwin Hawkins Singers, vocal performance of "Oh Happy Day", by Philip Dodson and Edward F. Rumbault, recorded 1990 on Oh Happy Day, Light Records. Compact disk.

21. Chris Tomlin, vocal performance of "I Will Rise", by Chris Tomlin and Louie Goglio, recorded 2008 on Hello Love, Sparrow Records-sixstepsrecords. Compact disk.

22. Chris Tomlin, vocal performance of "Jesus Messiah", by Daniel Carson, Ed Cash, and Chris Tomlin recorded 2011 on How Great is Our God: The Essential Collection, sixsteprecords/Sparrow Records. Compact disk.

23. Kari Jobe, vocal performance of "Be Still", by Kari Jobe, recorded 2009 on Be Still, Gateway Create Publishing. Compact disk.

24. Hillsong, vocal performance "Holy Spirit Rain Down", recorded 2010 on Touching Heaven Changing Earth, Hillsong Church T/A Hillsong Music. Compact disk.

25. Casting Crown, vocal performance, "While We Were Sleeping", by Mark Hall, recorded 2008 on Peace on Earth, Provident Label Group LLC, a unit of Sony Music Entertainment. Compact disk.

26. Guy Penrod, vocal performance, "Knowing You'll Be There", by Joan E. Wear, recorded 2005 on The Best of Guy Penrod, Spring House Music Group. Compact disk.

27. The Temptations, vocal performance, "My Girl", by Smokey Robinson and Ronald White, recorded 2002 on My Girl, Motown Records, a Division of UMG Recordings, Inc. Compact disk.

28. Martina McBride, vocal performance, "In My Daughter's Eyes", by James T. Slater and Don Hart, recorded 1995 In My Daughter's Eyes, on Martina, BMG Music. Compact disk.

29. Shane & Shane, vocal performance, "Blessed Assurance", by Fanny Crosby and Phoebe P. Knapp, recorded 2006

on Bluegrass Sample (Featuring the Peasall Sisters), IndependentBands.com. Compact disk.

30. Sissel, vocal performance, "My Tribute, To God Be the Glory", by Andrae Crouch, recorded 2006 on De Beste (1986-2006), Compact disk.

Author Note

I grew up in the small town of Wickes, Arkansas, on the farm my great-grandfather purchased many years ago. After high school, I attended Henderson State University and received a bachelors degree in elementary education, a masters degree in counseling, and a certificate from the Arkansas Department of Education to be a school administrator. I worked as an elementary teacher, school counselor, and as a school and college administrator until I retired in 2011. I live in Van Buren, Arkansas, with my husband Merle Dickerson. He serves as the superintendent of the Van Buren Public School District, so we continue to live with thoughts of children and how we can improve their future. To me, Van Buren is the perfect place to live.

I enjoyed working in education, surrounded by young ones. My greatest desire in life, or who I was meant to be, was the mother of a child. God answered my every prayer when He sent a precious baby girl with beautiful blond hair and sparkling blue eyes to me. She was named Amber CarLeigh. Like her name, Amber, she brought sunshine wherever she went. She was a happy child and participated in many school and church activities. Our days were never boring. We were always busy with church, school, and family activities.

Amber grew up sharing my belief in God and knowing that He is our Father in heaven.

I was blessed to be Amber's mother. She called me Mama, Mom, and Mother, all names precious to my heart. Amber grew up, went to college, fell in love, and married a young cattle rancher from southwest Arkansas. Amber was living back in cattle country and she loved it. Her horses were treated as her children and she loved them. Soon Amber became the mother of a little boy she named Brentley. On the day he was born I became a lovely new name, Nana. Suddenly I knew why our language includes the word *grandparent*. It is a "grand" feeling to be Brentley's Nana. Little Brentley stole our hearts from the beginning. He is so much like his mother but 100 percent pure boy. Life was beautiful.

Amber and I had a special bond. She was my only child and my best friend. She was the one with whom I shared all my secrets. We made up life's rules as we lived. We shared a love language where we could communicate easily with few words or none at all. We talked openly from the beginning. We had fun on purpose and wherever we could find it. When we parted, our last words were always, "I love you." I thank God that we could look directly into each other eyes and say those words out loud and mean them with all our hearts. I cannot imagine a more precious life filled with ordinary miracles.

CPSIA information can be obtained at www.ICGtesting.com
Printed in the USA
LVOW11s0905060914

402694LV00001B/25/P